Key Concepts in Primary Science

Audit and Subject Knowledge

CRITICAL
TEACHING

You might also like the following books from Critical Publishing:

Digital Literacy for Primary Teachers
Moira Savage and Anthony Barnett
978-1-909682-61-0 In print

Inclusive Primary Teaching: A critical approach to equality and special educational needs and disability, second edition
Janet Goepel, Helen Childerhouse and Sheila Sharpe
978-1-910391-38-9 In print

Learning Teaching: Becoming an inspirational teacher
Pete Boyd, Barry Hymer and Karen Lockney
978-1-909682-45-0 In print

Practical Ideas for Teaching Primary Science
Vivian Cooke and Colin Howard
978-1-909682-29-0 In print

Reflective Primary Teaching
Tony Ewens
978-1-909682-17-7 In print

Our titles are also available in a range of electronic formats. To order please go to our website www.criticalpublishing.com or contact our distributor, NBN International, 10 Thornbury Road, Plymouth PL6 7PP, telephone 01752 202301 or email orders@nbninternational.com

Key Concepts in Primary Science

Audit and Subject Knowledge

VIVIAN COOKE & COLIN HOWARD

CRITICAL
TEACHING

First published in 2016 by Critical Publishing Ltd

British Library Cataloguing in Publication Data
A CIP record for this book is available from the British Library

ISBN: 978-1-910391-50-1

This book is also available in the following e-book formats:

MOBI ISBN: 978-1-910391-51-8
EPUB ISBN: 978-1-910391-52-5
Adobe e-reader ISBN: 978-1-910391-53-2

Text design by Greensplash Limited
Cover design by Out of House Ltd
Project Management by Out of House Publishing
Printed and bound in Great Britain by Bell & Bain, Glasgow

Critical Publishing
152 Chester Road
Northwich
CW8 4AL
www.criticalpublishing.com

Contents

Acknowledgements

We are appreciative of the support from the University of Worcester and, in particular, the Institute of Education when writing this book. We are also grateful to our friends and science colleagues Karen Blackmore and Andy Plant who have helped to inspire us to write this text, which we hope will support our students when teaching science both while at university and in their future teaching careers.

We are extremely grateful to Julia Morris from Critical Publishing, whose editorial skills, critical feedback, patience and support has made this book possible.

Finally we would like to thank our immediate families for allowing us the time away from them, in particular Adrian, Adele, Isabella, Angela and Verity who have supported us on this journey.

Every effort has been made to trace copyright holders and to obtain their permission for the use of copyright materials. The publishers and authors will gladly receive information enabling them to rectify any error or omission in subsequent publications.

Meet the authors

Vivian Cooke is a principal lecturer in primary science within Initial Teacher Education at the University of Worcester and is also head of the Primary Centre. She began her teaching career as a primary school teacher with responsibility for science, design and technology, and information and communication technology. She has worked in two other higher education institutions as a senior lecturer in science on both postgraduate and undergraduate degree courses, as well as being the course leader for early years, primary and two-year PGCE courses.

Colin Howard is a senior lecturer in primary science within Initial Teacher Education at the University of Worcester. He has been involved in primary education for over 24 years, 14 of which were spent as a successful headteacher in both small village and large primary school settings. He has been involved in inspecting schools for the Diocese of Hereford as an S48 SIAS Inspector and has a strong research interest in the influence that school buildings have on their stakeholders.

1 Introduction: the importance of good subject knowledge

Who this book is for

This book has been written to enable trainee teachers on a university-based training route to develop a secure grasp of the primary science curriculum. It has also been designed to support more independent study for trainee teachers following any other alternative route into teaching such as School Direct or an assessment-only route. This book may also be useful if you are a recently qualified or qualified teacher.

Why this book is needed and chapter features

There is a growing body of research (Wellcome Trust, 2011; Ofsted, 2011, 2014) indicating that science, although now identified as a core subject, has a diminished profile in primary teaching (Ofsted, 2014). Recent Ofsted reports (Ofsted 2011, 2014) throw further light on the teaching of science by outlining the lack of specialist science knowledge among existing teachers.

This book has been written in response to these findings to allow you to develop an understanding of the concepts and knowledge outlined in the national curriculum for science at both Key Stages 1 and 2 (DfE, 2013). Given the importance of such statutory documents, each chapter starts with direct reference to this national framework. This will help you to develop your own knowledge of which aspects of science should be taught throughout each key stage. This book has also been written to encourage you to promote the successful delivery of primary science through creative, inspiring and practical lessons.

This book will help you to achieve Qualified Teacher status by enabling you to address aspects of the *Teachers' Standards* (DfE, 2013). In particular, it will help you meet Teachers' Standard 3, which requires you to demonstrate good subject and curriculum knowledge.

To be an outstanding teacher of primary science, you will be expected not only to have a strong subject knowledge, but also an understanding of children's ideas and possible misconceptions about science. Science includes a number of topics that are areas of weakness with many teachers – for example, topics in the physical sciences such as electricity and forces. This lack of subject knowledge will often result in children's misconceptions about science being left unchallenged in primary school, leading to the children making limited progress in their learning. It is also important that you can apply your subject knowledge in the classroom to make it accessible to the children you are teaching.

In addition to having a secure subject and pedagogical knowledge, it is vital that you develop an understanding of the nature, processes and methods of science. The national curriculum (DfE, 2013) describes this aspect of science as 'working scientifically' and states that this strand should not be taught separately, but should be embedded within the content of the other topics in the programme of study. Answers to scientific questions can be gleaned through the use of scientific enquiry, such as identifying, classifying and grouping, observing over time, pattern-seeking, researching and using secondary sources, as well as comparative and fair testing activities. Consideration of the need to work scientifically has therefore been embedded within the variety of practical activities offered within each chapter.

To allow you to become confident and competent in your science subject knowledge and subject-specific pedagogy, it is important that you are able to identify your strengths and areas of weakness. Therefore each chapter provides a subject knowledge audit to allow you to identify any gaps in your knowledge. This is then followed by a concept map of the key concepts dealt with in each chapter. The associated vocabulary is highlighted and the key concepts defined, together with examples. This is followed by an illustration of activities that can be used to teach the particular concept. At the end of each key concept, you are prompted to reflect on your understanding. A list of useful websites and further reading is given at the end of the book to provide you with the opportunity to develop your subject knowledge and understanding further. It is hoped that you will then revisit the initial subject audit and assess how your knowledge and understanding has improved in each area.

Chapter outlines

Chapter 1 – This introduction provides a discussion of the importance of good subject knowledge in the teaching of science. It provides information on the format of each chapter and the reasoning behind it.

Chapter 2 – Animals and humans – examines the factors that are essential for living organisms to develop, flourish and survive. It also covers aspects of life processes such as nutrition and basic physiology.

Chapter 3 – Plants, habitats and living things – explores the classification of living things, food chains, the growth of plants, the life cycle of flowering plants, and the functions and parts of a flower. Familiarising children with different classification keys is suggested, as well as making use of the outdoor world by visiting the local area and attempting to identify food chains. We suggest observing the germination of a seed and recording the changes using a diary, as well as using a digital microscope to observe the inside of bulbous plants. Finally, role play is promoted as a means of understanding pollination.

Chapter 4 – Evolution and inheritance – examines how humans and living things have evolved and adapted through time and how artificial and natural selection plays a vital role in evolution. It also looks at how the concept of the survival of the fittest and how such changes through the generations have made them dominant in a particular environment. It also considers the role of the fossil record in investigating how living things have evolved over time.

Chapter 5 – Everyday materials and their properties – looks at the concepts of the physical and chemical properties of materials, changes of shape, the particulate nature of matter, solid, liquids and gases, changes of state, dissolving and chemical change. Suggestions are made for sorting activities, understanding mechanical change by modelling clay, and considering what happens when cornflour is mixed with water. Working with ice balloons to understand melting and freezing and devising fair tests to consider which type of sugar will dissolve the fastest are suggested as activities. Making popcorn to explore chemical change is also featured.

Chapter 6 – Earth and space – explores the concept of the Moon, the Sun and stars, seasons, planetary motion, the solar system, and day and night. It describes how to teach children about the different time zones on Earth and recording the passage of time. It suggests keeping a Moon diary and making collages with pupils to help them understand the seasons. It prompts you to use secondary sources of information with your pupils to find out about different constellations and different models of the solar system that have been suggested in the past.

Chapter 7 – Rocks – covers the origins of rocks and soils and provides an understanding of the variety of rock types that exist on Earth. It considers the many and varied life forms that have lived on Earth and how a record of their existence may be found in the fossil record. It also provides an understanding of the processes of weathering and erosion that have helped shape the Earth.

Chapter 8 – Light – focuses on the sources of light and how light travels. It has been devised to help you teach about how we see light and how natural phenomena such as shadows are created. It encourages consideration of the properties of reflections and how light can be bent. Finally, it looks at colours and how rainbows are formed.

Chapter 9 – Forces, motion and magnets – promotes an understanding of the main concepts associated with forces such as friction and gravity. It considers what a force is, how forces are quantified and how objects are affected by resistant forces. Levers, pulleys and gears are studied to show how forces can be applied to our everyday lives. Magnets are also examined, including the forces they apply to each other and to some metals.

Chapter 10 – Sound – explores how sounds are created and how they reach our ears. It promotes an understanding of the key ideas associated with sound, such as pitch and loudness, and how they can be varied. Finally, alongside an exploration of our hearing, it considers how echoes are created and used to benefit humans and other animals.

Chapter 11 – Electricity – describes what electricity is and discusses series circuits, conductors and insulators, voltage and static electricity. It asks you to think about the uses of electricity and gives suggestions for making series circuits, incorporating conductors and insulators, and changing the voltage and resistance. There is a suggestion for lessons using secondary sources of information to research thunder and lightning.

Summary

In summary, this book:

- encourages you to audit your subject knowledge over a range of scientific topics;

- provides the required subject knowledge to teach the national curriculum at Key Stages 1 and 2 (DfE, 2013);

- highlights and defines essential scientific terminology;

- illustrates how concepts can be taught in practice through examples;

- encourages you to reflect on and develop your subject knowledge by directing you to further reading sources and websites.

References

Department for Education (DfE) (2013) *Teachers' Standards*. Available at: www.gov.uk/government/ uploads/system/uploads/attachment_data/file/301107/Teachers__Standards.pdf (accessed 10 July 2015).

Department for Education (DfE) (1999) *Science Programmes of Study for Key Stage 1 and Key Stage 2*. Available at: www.gov.uk/government/publications/science-programmes-of-study-for-key- stage-1-and-2-until-july-2015 (accessed 10 July 2015).

Ofsted (2011) *Successful Science*. Available at www.ofsted.gov.uk/sites/default/files/documents/ surveys-and-good-practice/s /Successful%20science.pdf (accessed 24 March 2015).

Ofsted (2014) *Maintaining Curiosity: a Survey into Science Education in Schools*. Available at: www.ofsted.gov.uk/resources/maintaining-curiosity-survey-science-education-schools (accessed 27 August 2015).

Wellcome Trust (2011) *Primary Science Survey Report*. London: Wellcome Trust.

2 Animals and humans

What do you need to know to be able to teach this topic?

Key Stage 1 of the national curriculum (DfE, 2013) states that children should be taught to:

-   *describe and compare the structure of a variety of common animals (fish, amphibians, reptiles, birds and mammals, including pets)*

-   *identify, name, draw and label the basic parts of the human body and say which part of the body is associated with each sense*

    (DfE, 2013: 149)

-   *find out about and describe the basic needs of animals, including humans, for survival (water, food and air)*

-   *describe the importance for humans of exercise, eating the right amounts of different types of food and hygiene*

-   *notice that animals, including humans, have offspring which grow into adults*

    (DfE, 2013: 152)

In Key Stage 2 of the national curriculum (DfE, 2013), teaching should:

-   *identify that animals, including humans, need the right types and amount of nutrition, and that they cannot make their own food; they get nutrition from what they eat*

-   *identify that humans and some other animals have skeletons and muscles for support, protection and movement*

    (DfE, 2013: 158)

–   describe the simple functions of the basic parts of the digestive system in humans

–   identify the different types of teeth in humans and their simple functions

(DfE, 2013: 162)

–   describe the life processes of reproduction in some plants and animals

–   describe the changes as humans develop to old age

(DfE, 2013: 168)

–   identify and name the main parts of the human circulatory system, and describe the functions of the heart, blood vessels and blood

–   recognise the impact of diet, exercise, drugs and lifestyle on the way their bodies function

–   describe the ways in which nutrients and water are transported within animals, including humans

(DfE, 2013: 172).

SUBJECT KNOWLEDGE AUDIT

Use the following audit to identify the strengths and areas for development in your subject knowledge of this topic.

Using a scale of 1–4, rate your current level of competence:

1 = Excellent; 2 = Good; 3 = Satisfactory; 4 = Needs improvement.

	1	2	3	4
Name the seven life processes associated with living things				
Explain the purpose of the heart				
Define the major vocabulary associated with blood vessels				
Explain the purpose of a skeleton for animals and humans				
Describe the role of joints and muscles in animals and humans				
Define the variety of muscles found in the body				
Name the parts of the digestive system				

Explain how the digestive system works				
Name the different types of teeth in humans				
Explain the role of each type of teeth				
Explain why living things need a healthy diet and exercise				

ANIMALS AND HUMANS: CONCEPT MAP

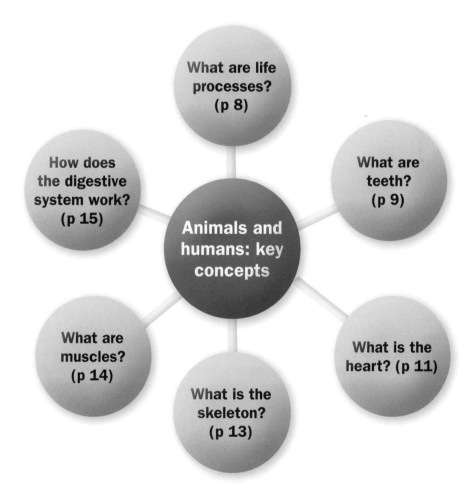

Key concept: what are life processes?

Associated vocabulary

ageing, amphibians, birds, cells, excretion, fish, glucose, growth, hearing, life expectancy, life processes, mammals, nutrition, reproduction, reptiles, respiration, sensitivity, sight, smell, species, taste, touch

---

Definitions

Life processes are the processes that define living things as being alive. These life processes include movement, **respiration, sensitivity, growth, reproduction, excretion** and **nutrition.** This can be remembered by the acronym MRS GREN (see Figure 2.1).

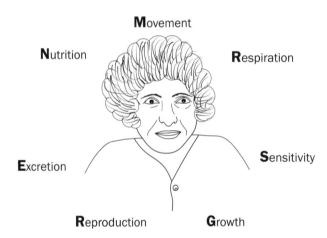

Movement

Nutrition

Respiration

Excretion

Sensitivity

Reproduction

Growth

Figure 2.1 *MRS GREN.*

Examples

From an early age, children become aware of the variety of life and the existence of common animals such as **fish, amphibians, reptiles, birds** and **mammals.** However, they need to understand that common life processes define a creature as living. Key facts include the following:

- Respiration involves a chemical reaction in **cells** that releases energy from **glucose** to allow cells to function properly.

- Senses such as **touch, taste, smell, hearing** and **sight** enable living things to be sensitive to their immediate environment.

- Living things have a finite **life expectancy**.

- The process of growth can be seen by changes to the bodies of living things and the **ageing** process, which, in humans, is typified by the greying of hair and the diminishing function of organs and senses.

- Although things are destined to die, it is important to realise that both plants and animals reproduce, replicating themselves, so that their **species** can continue to exist.

- By taking in substances that provide nutrition, living things are provided with the energy and nutrients necessary to sustain them and to allow life to flourish.

- This valuable nutrition is absorbed by the bodies of all living things and the waste products are excreted so that toxins do not build up.

- Humans and animals need exercise to keep healthy and fit. A healthy lifestyle increases life expectancy, but taking drugs such as alcohol and nicotine can damage organs and reduce life expectancy in humans.

In practice

Year 2

Pupils can undertake the following activity to gain an understanding of what life processes are necessary to decide whether things are living or not. Ask pupils to imagine they are aliens landing on our planet. How might they tell if a tree is alive compared with, say, a car. Allow them time to discuss this idea and reach their own conclusions of what is necessary for things to be classified as living. Next, ask the pupils to make a list of five other objects that the alien might encounter and again ask them to consider how the aliens might classify them. Provide pupils with a card with an image of MRS GREN on it as shown in Figure 2.1. They can use her to help them check whether their original ideas were correct. You might want to explain some of the more technical terms for them.

Check your understanding

1. Can you name the seven processes associated with living things?
2. Can you describe what each process involves?

Key concept: what are teeth?

Associated vocabulary

canines, dentine, enamel, erupt, gums, incisors, milk teeth, molars, nerves, permanent teeth, plaque, pre-molars, pulp, teeth, teething, tooth decay, wisdom teeth

Definitions

Human and animal **teeth** are located within their **gums**, which can be found in the upper and lower jaws. Teeth are used to mechanically break down food by crushing or cutting it up to speed up its later digestion in the stomach. They are made from a hard outer layer of **enamel** made predominately of calcium phosphate. This covers a layer of living cells called **dentine** and the innermost layer called the **pulp**, which contains blood vessels and **nerves**.

Examples

Young humans develop **milk teeth** first, which **erupt** out of the gums during **teething,** sometimes causing pain and discomfort. These 20 early teeth start to appear between six and 30 months of age and are then slowly replaced while children are at primary school by **permanent teeth.** These permanent teeth include:

*   **canines** for ripping and tearing;
*   **incisors** for biting and chewing;
*   **pre-molars** and **molars** for crushing and grinding food.

The molars also include **wisdom teeth**, which usually take longer to emerge and are often not seen until the late teens, or may not develop at all. Some animals have similar teeth to us; however, others, for example rodents, do not have incisors.

It is important that we brush our teeth from an early age to remove bacteria and the acids and sugars that are deposited on our teeth as a result of eating. These can build up to form a substance called **plaque**. If this is not removed, it will lead to the development of **tooth decay**. Regular visits to the dentist are necessary to maintain the health of our teeth.

In practice

Year 4

The following activity helps children to understand the value of brushing their teeth to remove acids. Provide them with some white wine vinegar in two small containers and two eggs, one of which has been left in a fluoride solution for ten minutes. Tell the children to place each egg into a container and to observe what happens. They should notice that the egg that has not been coated in fluoride will start to bubble as the acid in the vinegar attaches to the egg shell, while the other egg is resistant to such an attack.

You can then ask the children to consider why we have fluoride added to our water and toothpaste, as well as asking them about their experiences of going to the dentist and the advice that dentists and hygienists offer about dental hygiene.

Check your understanding

1. Can you name the different types of teeth?

2. Can you describe the different functions of each type of tooth?

3. Can you explain why dental hygiene is important?

Key concept: what is the heart?

Associated vocabulary

arteries, blood, capillaries, cardiac muscle, cardiovascular system, chambers, cholesterol, donor, heart, heart transplant, lungs, oxyhaemoglobin, oxygen, platelets, pulse, stroke, veins, white blood cells

---

Definitions

The **heart** is a very strong **cardiac muscle** that pumps **blood** around the body. Your **pulse** indicates how fast your heart is beating, which depends on whether or not you are resting. Your heart consists of four **chambers**, two upper chambers and two lower chambers; these muscular chambers squeeze the blood into and out of your heart and then around your body. The vessels that transport blood away from the heart are called **arteries** and those that carry blood back towards the heart are called **veins**. Another type of vessel, called a **capillary**, connects our arteries to our veins.

Examples

From an early age children will have seen blood on cuts and grazes and will have noticed its red appearance. However, they may not have considered its purpose and the role of the heart in circulating blood around the body.

The **cardiovascular system** allows blood to be pumped away from our heart at high pressure via our arteries, so that it can travel around our body. It then returns to our heart under lower pressure in our veins. Capillaries allow oxygen and nutrients, along with waste products such as carbon dioxide, to be exchanged between our body cells and our blood. Special valves inside our heart help to manage this one-way flow of blood and stop it going the wrong way around our circulatory system. Our **lungs** are part of our breathing system and allow air to move in and out of our body. Our heart pumps blood to our lungs, where it picks up the **oxygen** we have inhaled to form **oxyhaemoglobin**. Our blood also contains **white blood cells**, which help to protect us from infection and disease, along with **platelets**, which help our blood to clot so we do not bleed to death if we cut ourselves.

If we eat too much fatty food our heart can struggle to pump effectively because our blood vessels can become narrowed as a result of high levels of **cholesterol** in our blood. This can lead to high blood pressure and other health problems such as a **stroke**. If our heart needs to be replaced because it is failing, then we can have a **heart transplant**, although the consent of the **donor** and their family is needed and there are risks from infection and the possible rejection of the replacement heart.

In practice

Year 6

To start a study of the heart, ask the children to first draw the size and position of a heart on an image of a torso, as shown in Figure 2.2. Locate it for them if they are having problems.

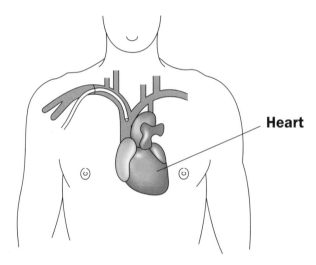

Figure 2.2 *Position of the human heart.*

To allow pupils to understand what the heart does, ask them to find their pulse, either by putting their index finger on the inside of their wrist or by feeling their neck just under their jawbone close to their ear. They can count the beats and calculate how many beats there are in a minute. Explain that this is a resting pulse rate because they are not exercising. Ask them to predict what would happen to their heart rate if they jogged on the spot, and why. Ask them to display their results using a line graph or a spreadsheet. Encourage them to discuss how their muscles work harder when they exercise so their heart beats faster to allow their blood to flow faster around their body, providing a greater supply of oxygen to their muscles.

Check your understanding

1. Can you define the major blood vessels associated with the heart?

2. Can you describe how the heart works?

3. Do you understand the effects of healthy eating and exercise on maintaining a healthy heart?

Key concept: what is the skeleton?

Associated vocabulary

backbone, ball and socket joint, bone, bone marrow, brain, chitin, exoskeleton, femur, greenstick fractures, hinge joint, hip, muscles, organs, pelvis, radius, rib cage, skeleton, skull, spinal cord, spine, tendons, ulna, vertebrae

---

Definitions

A **skeleton** is an internal or external structure made from a strong material such as **bone**. Its purpose is to support an animal or human, to facilitate movement and to protect internal tissues and **organs**.

Examples

- The **skull** houses and protects the **brain**.

- The **radius** and **ulna** are bones found in the arm.

- The **rib cage** protects the heart and lungs.

Through its many bones, the skeleton supports the weight of a human or animal as well as helping it to move. It also protects the **spinal cord**, which is responsible for carrying messages between the brain and other parts of the body – for example, the arms and legs. Movement in humans involves **tendons** and **muscles**, which are attached to joints – for example, the **ball and socket joint** attaching the **hips/pelvis** to the **femur** and the **hinge joint** found in the elbow. The **backbone** or **spine** is made up of **vertebrae.** Bones also serve as sites for the manufacture of red blood cells, platelets and white blood cells, which originate from the **bone marrow** in the centre of bones. Some children will have experienced a broken bone. These can be minor breaks such as **greenstick fractures**; more serious breaks can be repaired by setting them in a plaster cast.

Some animals, such as jellyfish, do not have a skeleton. Other creatures, such as crustaceans (eg crabs), have an **exoskeleton**. These external skeletons serve a similar purpose to our internal skeleton, but are made of a substance called **chitin** rather than bone.

In practice

Year 3

Find out whether pupils can identify a range of X-ray pictures (radiographs) taken of different bones. Explain to the pupils that not only do they need their bones to support their bodies, but that their bones are joined together at different types of joints. Ask the children to find a suitable space in which to move their legs and arms. First, ask them to explore how their upper leg and arm move in a circular motion. In discussion, encourage the children to realise that their hip and shoulder joints are both examples of ball and socket joints. Next, ask them to compare these movements with those in their knee and elbow joints. They will realise that these movements are predominantly hinge-like. Explain to the children that the knee and elbow are examples of hinge joints.

Check your understanding

1. Can you explain what role the skeleton plays in humans and other animals?

2. Can you name two major joints and where they can be found?

3. Can you name some bones found in a human skeleton?

4. How is an exoskeleton different from an internal skeleton?

Key concept: what are muscles?

Associated vocabulary

antagonistic pairs, biceps, cardiac muscles, fibres, involuntary muscles, muscles, skeletal muscles, smooth muscle, tendons, triceps, voluntary muscles

---

Definitions

Muscles are tissues composed of **fibres**. The contraction and expansion of these muscle fibres enable humans and other animals to move. Muscles are secured to our bones by **tendons**. Therefore they can only pull bones and allow us to move if they are part of a joint.

Examples

Skeletal muscles are attached to the bones of the skeleton and are **voluntary muscles** because we make them work by conscious thinking. Examples of these muscles include the **biceps** and **triceps**, which help to raise and lower our arms using our elbow joint. As the biceps muscle, which is located on the front of the upper arm, contracts, the triceps muscle relaxes and the forearm rises. This process is reversed to lower the arm again. These types of muscle are called **antagonistic pairs** because as one muscle contracts, the other relaxes.

Smooth muscles are **involuntary muscles** (they create automatic movements) and are found in the stomach wall, where they help us to digest food, and also in the iris of the eye, where they open and close our pupils. **Cardiac muscles** are involuntary muscles located around our heart. It is these muscles that produce the regular contractions of our heart.

In practice

Year 3

Ask pupils to tense and relax their upper arms so they can start to appreciate that they have muscles beneath their skin. These muscles are called the biceps (at the front of the upper arm) and the triceps (at the back of the upper arm). Ask them to measure the circumference of their upper arm when it is relaxed and then to measure it again when it is tensed. The children will note that the circumference increases when the biceps muscle is contracted.

Check your understanding

1. Can you explain what a muscle is?
2. Can you explain how muscles help us to move our limbs?

Key concept: how does the digestive system work?

Associated vocabulary

bile, carbohydrates, cud, digestion, digestive system, enzymes, excretion, faeces, gullet, hydrated, ingestion, large intestine, lipids, liver, minerals, nutrition, obese, oesophagus, proteins, ruminants, saliva, small intestine, stomach, urine, vitamins

---

Definitions

The **digestive system** includes a variety of organs and glands that allow the **ingestion**, **digestion** and absorption of food. The digestive system consists of the **oesophagus** or **gullet**, the **stomach**, the **small intestine** and the **large intestine**, which process our food so that we can derive **nutrition** from it.

Examples

From an early age children need to be taught about the value of food and water in their daily lives. However, as they move into Key Stage 2, this general awareness should be supplemented by a more detailed knowledge of the parts of the digestive system shown in Figure 2.3, their specific functions, and the types of food groups that sustain us.

The water we drink alongside our food keeps us **hydrated.** The food in our diet starts its digestive journey in our mouths. This food is moistened by **saliva** and is then physically broken up as we chew. This is important because it breaks down the food we eat into small pieces. This allows the **enzymes** in our digestive system to work on it more quickly. Once the food has passed down our gullet into our stomach, it enters our small intestine. It is here that the food is digested and nutrients are absorbed into our bloodstream. The food then passes into our large intestine where surplus water is reabsorbed back into our bodies. Undigested or waste food eventually undergoes excretion as **faeces** and **urine**. The **liver**

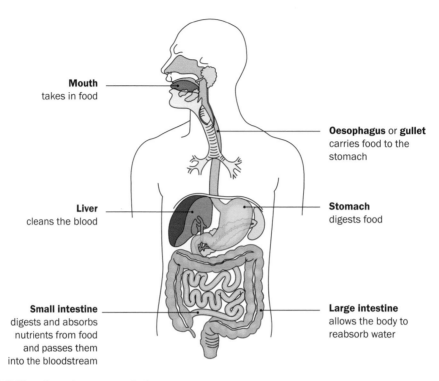

Mouth
takes in food

Oesophagus or **gullet**
carries food to the
stomach

Liver
cleans the blood

Stomach
digests food

Small intestine
digests and absorbs
nutrients from food
and passes them
into the bloodstream

Large intestine
allows the body to
reabsorb water

Figure 2.3 *The digestive system in humans.*

plays a fundamentally important role in the digestive system because it produces **bile**, which helps us digest fats and oils (known as **lipids**).

A healthy diet consists of a number of different types of food.

- **Carbohydrates**, such as pasta, provide our body with energy.
- Lipids (fats and oils), such as butter and olive oil, provide essential fatty acids and help in the absorption of some vitamins, as well as providing energy.
- **Proteins**, found in foods such as nuts and fish, help our bodies, bones and tissues to grow and repair.
- Small amounts of **vitamins** (eg vitamin D) and **minerals** (eg calcium) are essential in many different processes in our bodies.

If we do not eat healthily we can become too fat (**obese**) or thin and malnourished. A lack of certain vitamins and minerals can cause disease and ill-health.

Some living things have different digestive systems – for example, a cow has four parts to its stomach. To digest its food, a cow first swallows almost unchewed food, which passes into the first two parts of its stomach where it starts to ferment. The cow later coughs up this food or **cud** and thoroughly chews it, before it is again swallowed and enters the third and fourth parts of its stomach where it is finally digested. Animals that digest their food in this way are called **ruminants**.

In practice

Year 4

To help children to gain an idea of how the digestive system works, the following activity can be undertaken. Provide the children with scissors, a clear, strong, sealable bag, along with food items such as toast and a glass of squash.

- Ask the children to cut the toast up using scissors into smaller pieces and place it in the sealable bag. They should then squeeze the bag. Tell them that this stage represents the food being cut up and chewed into smaller pieces by their teeth.

- Then get them to pour the squash into the bag and seal it. They should squeeze the bag until the contents form a mushy-looking liquid. This part of the activity represents how food is liquefied by the action of the small intestine, which allows us to digest and absorb food into our bloodstream.

- Next, using a drawing pin, prick the bag and allow the liquid to drain out of the bag over a bowl or sink. This shows how our large intestine allows any surplus liquid water to be reabsorbed back into our bodies.

Tell the pupils that what is left in the bag are the waste products of digestion and that these, in turn, will be excreted from the body.

Check your understanding

1. Can you name the different parts of the digestive system?
2. Can you explain how the digestive system works?
3. Why is it important to eat a balanced diet?

3 Plants, habitats and living things

What do you need to know to be able to teach this topic?

The national curriculum (DfE, 2013) places a statutory requirement on schools to teach pupils about plants, habitats and living things. In Key Stage 1, pupils should be taught to:

- *identify and name a variety of common wild and garden plants, including deciduous and evergreen trees*

- *identify and describe the basic structure of a variety of common flowering plants, including trees*

(DfE, 2013: 148)

- *explore and compare the differences between things that are living, dead and things that have never been alive*

- *identify that most things live in habitats to which they are suited and describe how different habitats provide for the basic needs of different kinds of animals and plants, and how they depend on each other*

- *identify and name a variety of plants and animals in their habitats, including micro-habitats*

- *describe how animals obtain their food from plants and other animals, using the idea of a simple food chain, and identify and name different sources of food*

(DfE, 2013: 151)

- *observe and describe how seeds and bulbs grow into mature plants*

- *find out and describe how plants need water, light and a suitable temperature to grow and stay healthy*

(DfE, 2013: 152)

At Key Stage 2, pupils need to:

–   *identify and describe the functions of different parts of flowering plants: roots, stem/ trunk, leaves and flowers*

–   *explore the requirements of plants for life and growth (air, light, water, nutrients from soil, and room to grow) and how they vary from plant to plant*

–   *investigate the way in which water is transported within plants*

–   *explore the part that flowers play in the life cycle of flowering plants, including pollination, seed formation and seed dispersal*
                                                    (DfE, 2013: 157)

–   *recognise that living things can be grouped in a variety of ways*

–   *explore and use classification keys to help group, identify and name a variety of living things in their local and wider environment*

–   *recognise that environments can change and that this can sometimes pose dangers to living things*
                                                    (DfE, 2013: 161)

–   *describe the differences in the life cycles of a mammal, an amphibian, an insect and a bird*

–   *describe the life processes of reproduction in some plants and animals*
                                                    (DfE, 2013: 168)

–   *describe how living things are classified into broad groups according to common observable characteristics and based on similarities and differences, including micro-organisms, plants and animals*

–   *give reasons for classifying plants and animals based on specific characteristics*
                                                    (DfE, 2013: 172)

SUBJECT KNOWLEDGE AUDIT

Use the following audit to identify the strengths and areas for development in your subject knowledge of this topic.

Using a scale of 1–4, rate your current level of competence:

1 = Excellent; 2 = Good; 3 = Satisfactory; 4 = Needs improvement.

	1	2	3	4
Identify common and wild plants				
Define the terms deciduous and evergreen				
Describe the basic structure of flowering plants				
Know the difference between the phrases living, non-living and never been alive				
Understand what is meant by habitats and what living things live in them				
Know what a food chain is				
Describe the functions of different parts of flowering plants				
Know the differences between the conditions for germination of seeds and the growth of plants				
Know the life cycle of flowering plants, including pollination, seed formation and seed dispersal				
Be able to group different living things together based on observable and specific characteristics, similarities and differences using classification keys				
Understand that all animals, eg butterflies, have life cycles				
Describe the life processes of reproduction in some plants and animals				

PLANTS, HABITATS AND LIVING THINGS: CONCEPT MAP

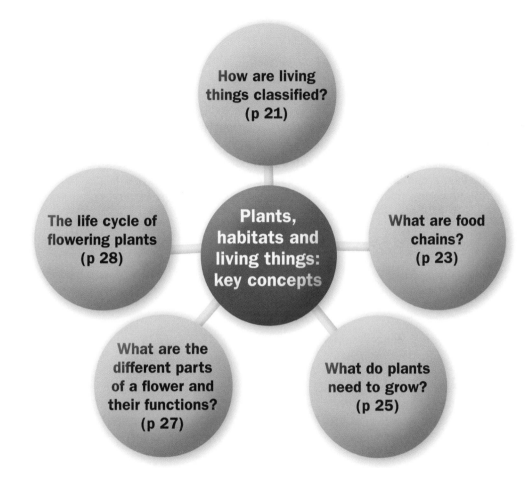

How are living things classified? (p 21)

The life cycle of flowering plants (p 28)

Plants, habitats and living things: key concepts

What are food chains? (p 23)

What are the different parts of a flower and their functions? (p 27)

What do plants need to grow? (p 25)

Key concept: how are living things classified?

Associated vocabulary

amphibians, animals, bacteria, birds, deciduous, evergreen, fish, fungi, invertebrates, kingdoms, living things, flowering, mammals, non-flowering plants, plants, protoctista, reptiles, vertebrates, viruses

Definitions

Living things are classified into groups based on their similarities and differences, which then allows us to identify them.

There are five **kingdoms** or large groups of living things:

- **animals**;

- **plants**;

- **fungi**;

- **protoctista**;

- **prokaryotes.**

The plant and animal kingdoms are further divided into progressively smaller groups with similar characteristics. For example, animals are divided into smaller groups such as **vertebrates** (with a backbone) and **invertebrates** (without a backbone). Vertebrates are further divided into **fish, amphibians, reptiles, birds** and **mammals**. Plants are divided into **flowering** and **non-flowering** plants and also into those that are **evergreen** (keep their leaves all year round) and **deciduous** (lose their leaves in winter).

Examples

Figure 3.1 illustrates the different groups of plants and animals.

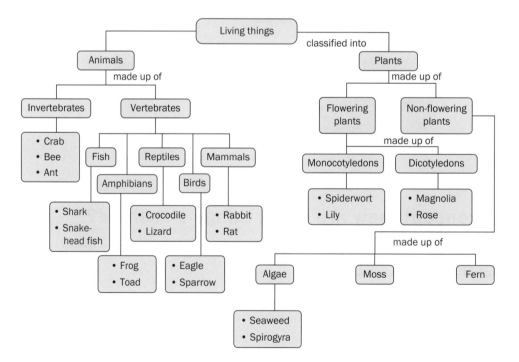

Figure 3.1 *Classification of plants and animals. Examples are marked by bullet points.*

In practice

Year 6

Explain how living things are grouped together based on their observable characteristics and similarities. Then provide the children with a plant classification key and pictures of different types of plants and ask them to use the key to identify common plants such as a fern or sunflower, or you could use real flowers if it is the right time of year.

If you have access to a pond, provide the pupils with a pond classification key and, after some pond dipping, ask them to identify and name any living things found in the pond. Do adhere to health and safety requirements and remember to return any living things back to the pond.

Check your understanding

1. Can you name the five kingdoms of living things?

2. Do you know the difference between flowering and non-flowering plants and can you give some examples of each?

3. Can you explain the difference between a deciduous and an evergreen plant?

4. Can you name the five groups of vertebrates and provide some examples of each?

Key concept: what are food chains?

Associated vocabulary

adapted, carnivores, community, consumers, food chain, habitat, herbivores, interdependent, micro-habitat, omnivores, photosynthesise, plant, populations, predators, prey, producers, species

Definitions

A **food chain** describes a feeding relationship in a **habitat** (the environment in which a particular plant or animal lives). A **micro-habitat** is a small part of that habitat. Different **species** often live in the same habitat – for example, a forest. A **community** refers to the different **populations** of species living together. The community will interact with the habitat in many different ways.

A food chain generally starts with a green **plant**. One exception is a geyser, where bacteria at the start of the food chain live on the chemicals in the volcanic water. The plants in a food chain are known as **producers** as they are the only living things that can **photosynthesise** and produce their own food. All other living things depend on plants for their food as they consume the food that the plants have produced, or the animals that have eaten those plants. They are thus known as **consumers.** Consumers can be **herbivores** if they only eat plants, **carnivores** if they only eat meat, or **omnivores** if they eat both plants and animals. **Predators** are animals that hunt and kill other animals for food. The **prey** is the resource for the predator. The prey always comes before the predator in a food chain and the energy is transferred from the prey to the predator.

Over time, living things can adapt to their environment, exhibiting either physical changes that help them to survive or live in that environment, or behavioural changes, such as animals living together in herds.

Examples

The short food chain below shows creatures that feed on other living things in a pond habitat. The pond weed is at the start of the food chain and is the producer. The arrows show the direction of energy flow.

Pond Weed $\longrightarrow$ Water Snail $\longrightarrow$ Fish $\longrightarrow$ Heron

(producer)   eaten by   eaten by   eaten by

In practice

Year 2

Take your pupils on a tour of the local park or other nearby habitat and ask them to identify the different plants and animals found there and think about how that environment provides their basic needs, such as water. Then ask them to think how the plants and animals that live in the habitat might have **adapted** to their environment. Return to school and ask the children to research, using books or websites, a particular animal or plant found in the park and its adaptations. Ask them to consider the different food chains that might exist in that habitat and the **interdependence** of living things. Question how the environment might change and how that could have an impact on the plants and animals found there – for example, the building of a housing estate.

Check your understanding

1. Can you give an example of a food chain and describe what is happening?

2. Do you know the difference between a predator and its prey?

3. Can you provide an example of how an animal has adapted to the environment in which it lives?

Key concept: what do plants need to grow?

Associated vocabulary

bulbs, carbon dioxide, chlorophyll, corms, embryo, germination, glucose, leaves, life cycle, light, nutrition, nutrients, oxygen, photosynthesis, plant, plumule, radicle, root, seed, shoot, stems, testa, trunk, tubers, water

---

Definitions

The **life cycle** of a **plant** begins with **germination**, which is when a **seed** absorbs water and its **embryo** swells and splits the **testa**. The **radicle** (the part of the plant embryo that develops into a root) then appears and grows downwards and the **plumule** (the part of the plant embryo that develops into a **shoot**) grows upwards. Seeds require water, oxygen and a suitable temperature to germinate.

Some plants, such as daffodils, grow from **bulbs**, which are underground root structures that contain a supply of food. Other plants, such as gladioli, grow out of **corms**, which are short, vertical, swollen underground plant **stems** that act as storage organs and are used by the plant to survive in adverse weather conditions, such as drought. Dahlias grow from **tubers**, which are enlarged fleshy stems that grow underground and sprout eyes that can grow into new plants.

Plants use **water** and **carbon dioxide** from the atmosphere and **light** from the Sun to photosynthesise and make their own food **(nutrition)**. Water and **nutrients** from the soil are transported through the **roots** of the plant, up the stem to the **leaves** (or **trunk** in a tree). The stem thus has the dual functions of holding the plant upright as well as spreading its leaves to allow photosynthesis to occur. Green plants absorb light energy from the Sun using **chlorophyll** in their leaves and the light energy is used in the reaction between **carbon dioxide** and **water** to produce **glucose** and **oxygen.** The glucose is used in respiration or converted into starch and stored. Oxygen is produced as a by-product. The process of **photosynthesis** is shown in the following diagram:

$$\text{carbon dioxide + water} \;—\; \text{Sun's energy} \;\longrightarrow\; \text{glucose + oxygen}$$

The rate of photosynthesis depends on the temperature, the concentration of carbon dioxide and the intensity of light.

Plants also use minerals or nutrients such as iron and magnesium from the soil for healthy growth.

Examples

Figure 3.2 shows the germination of a seed. Sunflower seeds, broad beans and cress seeds are examples of seeds that can be used to illustrate germination to children.

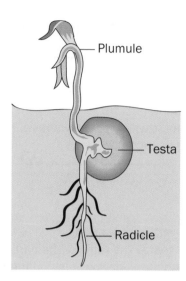

Figure 3.2 *Parts of a germinating seed.*

In practice

Year 2

Ask the children to place a bean seed on some cotton wool saturated with water. Ask them to take a photograph every day using a digital camera and to keep a diary describing what is happening to the seed. Alternatively, digital time-lapse software such as Windows Movie Maker can be used. Discuss the conditions that the bean requires for germination. Provide them with the appropriate scientific vocabulary, such as embryo, testa and plumule, so they can use these terms in their writing.

Offer different bulbous plants for the children to examine, such as tulips, daffodils, irises, hyacinths, onions, crocuses and lilies. Cut them open and allow the pupils to examine their insides using magnifying glasses or a digital microscope. Encourage pupils to plant their own bulbs, in the ground or in a container, under different conditions, including in the cold. Discuss the conditions that the bulbs require for growth and how the seasons affect plant growth – for example, spring-flowering bulbs are planted in the autumn because they need a period of cold weather to stimulate germination.

Check your understanding

1.   Can you describe the conditions required for germination to take place?

2.   How do seeds and bulbs grow into mature plants?

3.   Identify and describe the different parts and functions of a plant.

4.   What do plants need to grow and stay healthy?

Key concept: what are the different parts of a flower and their functions?

Associated vocabulary

anther, carpel, filament, nectar, nectaries, ovary, ovules, petals, pollen, receptacle, sepals, stamens, stigma, style

Definitions

A flower consists of different parts that perform specific functions.

Petals are often very brightly coloured because their main function is to attract insects, such as bees, into the flower. The insects pick up **pollen** from the flower and carry it to the next flower where pollination can occur.

Sepals are special types of leaves that form a ring around the petals. Their role is to protect the flower while it is still a bud. Once the flower has opened, the sepals can be seen behind the petals. Sepals are usually green or brown, but in some plants they are the same colour as the petals.

Nectaries, which are usually found in the centre of the flower, are the parts of the flower that make nectar. **Nectar** is a sweet substance that insects drink to give them energy. Bees use nectar to make honey.

The **carpel** is the female part of the flower where the seeds are made. The carpel has three parts: the **stigma,** the **style** and the **ovary**. The stigma is covered in a sticky substance that captures grains of pollen and the style is the stalk that holds the stigma up. The ovary contains the **ovules** or eggs.

The **stamens** are the male parts of the flower. Their role is to make pollen, a fine yellow powder needed to make a new plant. Each stamen has two parts, an **anther** and a **filament**. The anther contains the pollen and the filament holds the anther up.

The **receptacle** is the top part of the flower stalk, where the parts of the flower are attached, and is often rounded in shape. All the parts of the flower are attached to the receptacle.

Example

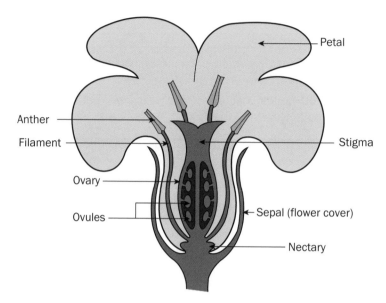

Figure 3.3 *Main parts of a flower.*

In practice

Year 3

Briefly explain the key points and functions of the petals, sepals, nectaries, style, stigma, ovaries, ovules, stamens, anther, filament and receptacle to the children. A diagram might be helpful. Children can then examine a flower, such as a tulip, and use a magnifying glass to identify the different parts. They can then draw and label what they have observed.

Check your understanding

1. Can you identify the different parts of a flowering plant?
2. Are you confident in describing the functions of each part of the flowering plant?
3. Can you explain why some flowers have brightly coloured petals?

Key concept: the life cycle of flowering plants

Associated vocabulary

asexual reproduction, anther, carpel, clones, cross-pollination, fertilisation, flower, fruit, germinate, life cycle, ovary, ovules, pollen, pollination, self-pollinate, seeds, seed formation, seed dispersal, stigma, style, vegetative reproduction

Definitions

Flowering plants have a **life cycle**, as shown in the following diagram:

Pollination ⟶ Fertilisation ⟶ Seed formation ⟶ Seed dispersal ⟶ Germination

Pollination occurs when **pollen** from an **anther** is carried to the **stigma** of a **flower**. Some flowers **self-pollinate** and pollen is carried to the stigma of the same plant. Other flowers **cross-pollinate** and pollen is carried to the stigma of another plant by the wind or insects.

When the pollen reaches the **carpel** of the new flower, it fertilises the egg cells in the **ovary** to make **seeds**. The pollen first sticks to the stigma and then travels down the **style** to the ovary. In the ovary, the pollen joins with the ovules and the **ovules** become seeds. This process is called **fertilisation.**

Each fertilised ovum develops into a seed containing a shoot, root, and one or two seed leaves. This is known as **seed formation**. The ovary containing the fertilised seeds will develop into a **fruit**. **Seed dispersal** occurs when the seeds are scattered by animals or the wind. Some of the seeds will **germinate** and grow into new plants.

Some plants reproduce by **asexual** or **vegetative reproduction**. Parts of the parent plant will separate to form new plants that are exactly the same as the parent plant.

Examples

Pollen grains can be carried by insects that have collected nectar from the plant – for example, pollen will stick to the bodies of bees and allow them to move pollen from one plant to another. Insect-pollinated flowers have large coloured petals to attract insects, are often sweetly scented and contain nectar. The anther and the stigma are often found inside the flower so that insects can brush against them and pick up the pollen.

Wind-pollinated flowers, in contrast, have small petals that are not brightly coloured and have no scent or nectar. The pollen is produced in large amounts because a large proportion of it does not reach another flower. The anther and the stigma hang outside the flower so that they can be blown in the wind. Dandelions and sycamore seeds are light and have extensions that act as parachutes or wings to catch the wind.

Plants such as tomatoes and plums have brightly coloured and succulent fruits that contain seeds with indigestible coats. This allows the seeds to pass undamaged through the digestive tracts of animals and they are dispersed when the animal excretes them. In other plants, such as peas, the seeds are found in pods that burst open when ripe, projecting the self-propelled seeds away from the plant.

Some plants reproduce asexually (ie without flowers or fertilisation). Two of the most important methods of asexual reproduction are runners (eg strawberry and spider plants) and tubers (eg potatoes and dahlias). Plants produced asexually are genetically identical to each other and to the parent – that is, they are **clones**.

In practice

Year 5

Play the following pollination game in the playground.

Equipment:

- T-shirts and antennae (worker bees);
- coloured squares (for different flowers, eg red squares for red flowers);
- margarine tubs (anthers);
- woolly socks over a hand (stigma);
- ping-pong balls with self-adhesive hooks (pollen grains).

Divide the children into two teams representing worker bees and flowers.

- The coloured squares can be pinned onto the children's clothes or PE vests to represent different flowers.
- Use the margarine tubs containing the pollen grains to represent the anthers (stamens) in each flower.
- Use the woolly sock over a hand to represent the stigmas in each flower.
- The ping-pong balls representing three pollen grains will stick to the woolly socks (stigmas).
- Each flower needs two or four pollen grains identified by the same coloured square.
- Each team of flowers lives in its own flower bed, which should be demarcated, as well as some hives.

Blow the whistle to start the game. The worker bees leave their hive and run to the flower bed to collect pollen from the different coloured flowers. As each worker bee visits a flower, it must collect two pollen grains. It must then return to the hive and deposit one pollen grain in the hive before visiting another flower. At the next flower, the bee deposits the second pollen grain on the woolly sock (stigma) and then collects two more pollen grains. The bee then takes one of these pollen grains to the hive and the second to another flower. The bees continue their activities (collecting and depositing pollen) until the whistle blows to stop the game after three minutes. Each team then counts the number of pollen grains that have been transferred to the hive for the bees and onto the sock. This will show that pollination has taken place and that the pollen has been transferred from anther to stigma. The team with the highest total score is the winner.

Check your understanding

1. Can you name the different stages of the life cycle of a flowering plant?
2. Are you confident in describing what happens in the different stages of the life cycle of a flowering plant?
3. Can you explain the differences between self-pollination and cross-pollination?
4. Can you define asexual or vegetative reproduction?

4 Evolution and inheritance

What do you need to know to be able to teach this topic?

The national curriculum (DfE, 2013) suggests that pupils in upper Key Stage 2 should be taught to:

- _identify that most living things live in habitats to which they are suited_

(DfE, 2013: 151)

- _identify how animals and plants are adapted to suit their environment in different ways and that adaptation may lead to evolution_
- _recognise that living things have changed over time and that fossils provide information about living things that inhabited the Earth millions of years ago_
- _recognise that living things produce offspring of the same kind, but normally offspring vary and are not identical to their parents_

(DfE, 2013: 173)

SUBJECT KNOWLEDGE AUDIT

Use the following audit to identify the strengths and areas for development in your subject knowledge of this topic.

Using a scale of 1–4, rate your current level of competence:

1 = Excellent; 2 = Good; 3 = Satisfactory; 4 = Needs improvement.

	1	2	3	4
Define the term evolution				
Define the term natural selection				
Explain the concept of the survival of the fittest				
Describe how genes can influence the development of individuals				
Explain why there is so much variation within living things				
Name scientists linked with the theory of evolution				

EVOLUTION AND INHERITANCE: CONCEPT MAP

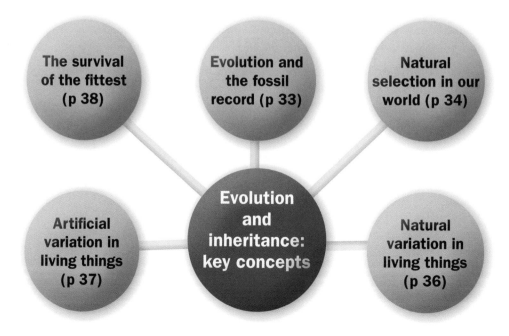

Key concept: evolution and the fossil record

Associated vocabulary

Charles Darwin, Cretaceous, dinosaurs, extinct, evolution, evolutionary history, fossil record, theory of evolution, trilobites

---

Definitions

Evolution is the theory that explains how living species have developed, adapted and changed over geological time.

Examples

Our understanding of the **theory of evolution** has been informed by seminal works by famous scientists such as **Charles Darwin**, who explained how different species have evolved over geological time from the simplest of organisms, such as the first bacteria that appeared around 3.5 billion years ago, to modern day humans. Some species, such as **trilobites**, that existed in the Earth's earliest history have become **extinct** as a result of competition from other species, changes in the Earth's environment, or during the mass extinctions found periodically throughout the geological record. For example, the **Cretaceous** period saw the demise of the **dinosaurs** at a time of mass extinction. Although these creatures are not now alive for us to examine, evidence of their early **evolutionary history** may be found in the **fossil record**. Unfortunately, we do not have a complete record of the evolutionary history of dinosaurs because the fossil record is incomplete. However, more complete evolutionary records exist for animals such as the horse. In this case, we can see how this species evolved into what we see today – for example, from having earlier multi-toed feet to the current single-toed hooves that allow horses to run more easily.

In practice

Year 6

For children to understand that we, as humans, have been around for only a very short period of evolution, you can ask the children to create their own evolutionary timeline. Take the children out to a large open space and provide them with a metre stick and labelled cards with the following words written on them:

- bacteria;
- early fish;
- first amphibians/insects/reptiles;
- dinosaurs;
- mammals and birds;
- modern day mammals;

- early humans/hominids;
- *Homo sapiens*/Neanderthals;
- modern day humans.

Provide the children with the following table:

Distance	Species/event
22.5m	Creation of the Earth
17.5m	Bacteria
2.5m	Early fish
1.95m	First amphibians, insects, reptiles
1.1m	Dinosaurs
1m	Mammals and birds
22.5cm	Modern day mammals
1.5mm	Early humans/hominids
1mm	*Homo sapiens*, Neanderthals
0	Modern day humans

Ask the children to measure from a fixed point to the distances given in the table, placing the relevant card at the point of each measurement. Once they have completed this activity, the children will be surprised how long evolution has lasted compared with the emergence of modern day humans. You could also ask the pupils to research the groups of species outlined in this task so they can see what they looked like.

Check your understanding

1. Can you define evolution?

2. Can you describe some species in the Earth's evolutionary history?

3. Can you name creatures that can be linked to different geological eras (eg dinosaurs and trilobites)?

Key concept: natural selection in our world

Associated vocabulary

adaptation, Alfred Wallace, antibodies, antibiotics, antibiotic-resistant strains, bacteria, Charles Darwin, evolve, genes, habitat, selective advantage, viruses

Definitions

Individuals in a species show an extensive range of variation as a result of differences in their **genes**. Natural selection takes place when an individual has a **selective advantage** over the rest of their species as a result of these genetic variations. When these individuals reproduce, they will pass on to their offspring the genes that made them more successful and prolific. Over time, this will lead to the unsuccessful individuals of the species dying out and the more successful individuals becoming dominant. The species as a whole will therefore **evolve** and survival rates will increase.

Examples

Charles Darwin was an English naturalist. In 1859, in his famous book *On the Origin of Species*, he proposed that evolution was the result of natural selection. Pupils may have also come across other important figures in this field, such as **Alfred Wallace**.

Pupils may already have started to recognise how natural selection in animals has led them to respond to their environment, such as the long necks of giraffes enabling them to eat leaves from high branches, or the stripes of tigers providing camouflage. All such **adaptations** have resulted in these animals surviving and flourishing in a particular **habitat**.

Micro-organisms such as **bacteria** and **viruses** can also adapt and, because they reproduce very rapidly, this means that they can evolve over short periods of time. The human body is always producing new **antibodies** to fight new viruses and scientists need to continuously develop new **antibiotics** to fight **antibiotic-resistant strains** of bacteria.

In practice

Year 6

Observe the variety of birds in the school grounds and ask the children to consider how their beaks have evolved and adapted to suit a variety of tasks and food sources. The following activity will reinforce this idea.

Provide each child with a series of small pots, each with some of the following items in it:

- sunflower seeds;
- some cress or blanket weed in water;
- some grains of rice set in jelly.

Give each child some tweezers, a pair of pliers and a small tea strainer. Ask them which tool would be best suited to collect each food type if they represented a bird's beak. The pliers can open the sunflower seeds, the tweezers can pick up the rice and the sieve is best used to remove the blanket weed or cress from the water. Explain that each tool is like a beak for a particular species of bird and that each beak has evolved to be best suited for a particular purpose. In this case, the pliers are like the beak of a sparrow or parrot, the sieve behaves like a duck's bill and the tweezers represent a woodpecker's beak.

Check your understanding

1. Can you define natural selection?

2. Can you describe some examples of natural selection?

3. Complete an audit of the types of birds found in your school grounds and their beak shapes to help you teach this topic.

Key concept: natural variation in living things

Associated vocabulary

cells, DNA, genetic inheritance, random mutations

Definitions

Natural variation within a species occurs when there are differences within a population of individuals. These differences may be due to the **genetic inheritance** passed down from the individual's parents, **random mutations** in the **DNA** present in **cells**, or alterations to a cell's DNA resulting from environmental causes.

Examples

Children can look a bit like their father and a bit like their mother, but they will never be exactly identical to either of their parents. This is because they inherit a mixture of traits from each parent when their genes are passed on at conception. Genes are short sections of DNA. They are genetic building blocks and contain the instructions needed to build living cells. Different genes determine the natural variations that occur in the colour of children's hair and eyes and also determine whether they are male or female. Some diseases, such as the blood disorder sickle cell anaemia, are caused when a particular genetic variation is passed down from both parents to a child. The genetic code is copied each time a cell divides and random mutations or changes can occur in DNA over time.

Some characteristics of animals and plants can be affected by environmental changes. For example, some hydrangeas develop blue flowers in acidic soils and pink flowers in alkaline soils.

In practice

Year 6

To discover how genes can randomly create a variety of different humans, ask children to play this simple game. First, give them a drawing of a human that looks like either the man or the woman described in the table below.

Trait	Woman (mother)	Man (father)
Face shape	H = round	T = oval
Eye shape	H = circular	T = oval
Hairstyle	H = wavy	T = straight
Mouth	H = large lips	T = narrow lips
Ear	H = pointed	T = normal
Nose	H = straight and thin	T = bulbous
Eye colour	H = blue	T = green
Neck	H = long and thin	T = short
Freckles	H = no freckles	T = lots of freckles

Next, tell the children that they are going to create a drawing that will represent an example of the offspring from this mother and father. However, tell them that the traits of both the mother and the father will be passed on by randomly tossing a coin. Give each child a piece of paper and each pair of children a coin. Tell them that if they toss a head (H), they get a personal trait from the mother's column and if they toss a tail (T) they get the trait from the father's column. When they get this trait they must draw it. The children will quickly grasp that some traits of the child are from the mother and some are from the father.

Check your understanding

1. Can you explain what natural variation is and why/how it occurs?

2. Can you explain what DNA is?

Key concept: artificial variation in living things

Associated vocabulary

artificial variation, breeds, cross-breeds, hybrids, pedigree dogs, selective breeding

Definitions

Artificial variation occurs when people use **selective breeding** to create new varieties of a species to promote a valued trait in that species.

Examples

Artifical variation has been used for a long time in animals such as dogs to speed up evolutionary changes within the species. It has led to the large range of sizes and shapes now available through what are called **breeds,** such as Dalmations and dachshunds. Although dogs are the same species, different types have been produced by selective breeding.

More recently, selective breeding has been used to promote advantageous traits for us as humans, such as an increased milk yield in cows, or even to remove certain disadvantageous genetic traits, such as a large muzzle in a dog.

In practice

Year 6

Give the children a range of photographs of different **pedigree dogs** and ask them to consider their specific characteristics. As some pupils will have their own dogs, they will no doubt end up talking about **cross-breeds** and how they represent a mix of two or more types of dog. Ask the children what makes their dog identifiable as a cross-breed rather than a pure breed or pedigree. To follow on from this, talk about unusual mixes of animals or **hybrids**, such as a tigon, which is the offspring of a tiger and a lion. Explore possible combinations of hybrid creatures by giving them a bag of laminated pictures of the pieces of two distinct, but similar, animals such as a donkey and a zebra. Give them items such as the tail, torso, legs, feet, eyes, ears and face shape and see what random hybrid creatures they can create.

Check your understanding

1. Can you explain what artificial variation is?

2. Can you explain why we have different breeds of dogs?

3. Can you provide any examples of the impact that artificial variation has had on our daily lives?

Key concept: the survival of the fittest

Associated vocabulary

evolutionary advantage, extinction, survival of the fittest

Definitions

The term **survival of the fittest** suggests that a species has changed and adapted over time so that it is best suited to a particular environment. Its origins are linked to the theory of evolution and it is the method by which natural selection occurs.

Examples

Evolutionary change occurs over many generations so it can be hard to see the adaptations that have led to the species alive today. However, if you help children to consider how they are different from the earliest forms of humans, then they will realise that they, as humans, are slowly evolving and changing over sustained periods of time, just like plants and other animals.

For humans and animals, changes in their physical and behavioural characteristics have provided them with **evolutionary advantages**, which have enabled them to survive more successfully than their predecessors in a variety of environments. For example, finches in the Galapagos Islands have evolved to have a variety of different beak shapes and sizes so they can survive in both the rainy and drought-like conditions found in their climate. Unfortunately, if a species cannot adapt quickly enough to sudden changes in their environment, this may lead to their extinction. An example is the dodo, whose population on the island of Mauritius was decimated when rats arrived on board visiting boats. The dodo laid their eggs in nests near to the ground and the eggs were eaten by the newly arrived rats, ultimately leading to the **extinction** of this bird before it could adapt by building its nests somewhere safer.

In practice

Year 6

To help children understand how a change in behaviour can benefit a species, ask them to fill up two small plastic bottles with warm water. Tell them to record the temperature of both these bottles. Place the first bottle somewhere draughty or on a cold surface outside, leaving it for 15 minutes. Place the other bottle in the same place, but this time stand it on a 1cm thick piece of polystyrene wrapped in bubble wrap. After 15 minutes, ask them to record the new temperatures of the bottles. Ask the children to consider what would happen if this was a penguin's egg that had been laid in Antarctica. Would the insulated egg have an advantage over the unprotected egg? You can then explain to the children that for Emperor penguins to hatch their chicks, they hold their solitary egg on their feet off the ground and cover it with a warm layer of feathered skin called a brood pouch. This allows their chicks to survive and flourish in this harsh environment.

Check your understanding

1. Can you explain what survival of the fittest means?
2. Can you explain some adaptations that animals or plants have made to give them an evolutionary advantage?
3. Can you research any other species that may have adapted to best survive in a particular habitat?

5 Everyday materials and their properties

What do you need to know to be able to teach this topic?

The national curriculum (DfE, 2013) places a statutory requirement on schools to teach pupils about materials and their properties. It suggests pupils should be taught to:

- distinguish between an object and the material from which it is made

- identify and name a variety of everyday materials, including wood, plastic, glass, metal, water, and rock

- describe the simple physical properties of a variety of everyday materials

- compare and group together a variety of everyday materials on the basis of their simple physical properties

(DfE, 2013: 149)

- identify and compare the suitability of a variety of everyday materials, including wood, metal, plastic, glass, brick, rock, paper and cardboard for particular uses

- find out how the shapes of solid objects made from some materials can be changed by squashing, bending, twisting and stretching

(DfE, 2013: 153)

- compare and group materials together, according to whether they are solids, liquids or gases

- observe that some materials change state when they are heated or cooled, and measure or research the temperature at which this happens in degrees centigrade (°C)

- identify the part played by evaporation and condensation in the water cycle and associate the rate of evaporation with temperature

(DfE, 2013: 162)

- compare and group together everyday materials on the basis of their properties including their hardness, solubility, transparency, conductivity (electrical and thermal) and responses to magnets

- know that some materials will dissolve in liquid to form a solution, and describe how to recover a substance from a solution

- use knowledge of solids, liquids and gases to decide how mixtures might be separated including through filtering, sieving and evaporating

- give reasons, based on evidence from comparative and fair tests, for the particular uses of everyday materials, including metals, wood and plastic

- demonstrate that dissolving, mixing and changes of state are reversible changes

- explain that some changes result in the formation of new materials, and that this kind of change is not usually reversible, including changes associated with burning and the action of acid on bicarbonate of soda

(DfE, 2013: 169)

SUBJECT KNOWLEDGE AUDIT

Use the following audit to identify the strengths and areas for development in your subject knowledge of this topic.

Using a scale of 1–4, rate your current level of competence:

1 = Excellent; 2 = Good; 3 = Satisfactory; 4 = Needs improvement.

	1	2	3	4
Distinguish between an object and the material it is made of				
Be able to describe the physical properties of materials				
Understand the differences between solids, liquids and gases				
Explain what happens when materials are heated or cooled				
Understand the processes of evaporation and condensation				
Know what happens when a material dissolves				
Understand how mixtures can be separated				
Know the differences between reversible and irreversible changes				

MATERIALS AND THEIR PROPERTIES: CONCEPT MAP

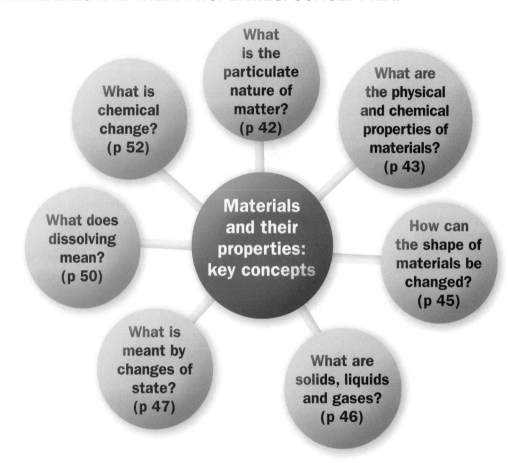

Key concept: what is the particulate nature of matter?

Associated vocabulary

atoms, compound, element, kinetic theory, molecule, oxygen, particles, water

Definitions

Atoms are the basic building blocks of matter. Atoms are the simplest type of particle and all matter is made of atoms. An **element** is a substance that cannot be broken down into a simpler substance and is made up of only one type of atom. When two or more atoms of the same or different elements combine to form a **molecule**, they form chemical bonds with each other. A molecule is the smallest particle of a substance that still retains all the properties of that substance. A **compound** is the name given to a substance that contains atoms of two or more different elements combined.

The **kinetic theory** of matter states that everything is made up of continually moving **particles** that are too small to see.

Examples

Scientists currently know of 118 different elements. These elements can be arranged on a diagram called a periodic table. Elements such as gold, silver, copper and carbon have been known for thousands of years, whereas other elements such as meitnerium, darmstadtium and ununquadium have only recently been created by scientists. Most elements occur naturally in the Earth's crust or atmosphere. Most of the elements are solid metals, such as copper. Mercury is the only liquid metal. Carbon is a non-metallic solid. Some elements, such as nitrogen, are gases.

Oxygen consists of molecules made from pairs of oxygen atoms. **Water** molecules are made up of two hydrogen atoms and one oxygen atom chemically bonded together. Water is called a compound because it is made up of two types of atoms from two different elements.

In practice

Particle theory is not part of the curriculum for Key Stage 2, but an understanding of the particulate nature of matter is important for you to be able to explain concepts such as changes of state and reversible and irreversible change.

Check your understanding

1. Can you explain the difference between an atom and a molecule?
2. Are you confident about explaining kinetic theory?
3. Do you know what elements and compounds are and can you define them?

Key concept: what are the physical and chemical properties of materials?

Associated vocabulary

chemical properties, conductivity, density, hardness, manufactured, melting point, physical properties, raw materials, strength, substance

Definitions

Materials are all around us. An object such as a table is made from a material or **substance.** Some materials, such as wood, occur naturally and are known as **raw materials**. Other materials, such as glass, are made or **manufactured** by people.

The **physical properties** of materials include their **hardness** (a hard material is rigid and resistant to pressure), **strength** (a strong material can withstand a force), **melting point** (the temperature at which a material changes from a solid to a liquid), **conductivity** (thermal or electrical) and **density** (the relationship between mass and volume).

The **chemical properties** of a material characterise how it responds during a chemical reaction which changes it – for example, the material may burn, corrode, or react with water. We choose the materials used for different purposes based on their physical and chemical properties.

Examples

Metals such as iron or copper are derived from ores found in rocks present in the Earth's crust. Metals are typically hard and strong, have a high density and good thermal and electrical conductivity. We build bridges from iron and steel because of these physical properties.

Glass is made from clay, sand and other minerals. Glass is hard and brittle with a medium density. It has a very high melting point and it is very unreactive – that is, it does not burn. We use glass for window panes and decorative items.

Plastics such as polythene are manufactured from crude oil (a raw material). Plastics are flexible, have a low density, are easily moulded and coloured, are poor conductors and can be transparent. Plastics melt and may burn on heating. We use plastics for making bottles because they are of low density and are easily moulded into the desired shape.

In practice

Year 1

Present children with a collection of everyday objects made from different materials – for example, a sock, wooden spoon, glass bottle, plastic mug and polythene bag. Ask them to identify the object and then the material that the object is made from. Talk about whether the substance or material from which the object was made occurs naturally or has been manufactured. Provide them with a list of vocabulary (eg strong, soft, hard, smooth, transparent) to help them identify and describe the physical properties of the objects. Ask them to sort the objects according to their different physical properties by placing them into labelled hoops (eg hard and soft). Prompt them to think about why these materials are suitable to make these particular objects.

Year 4

In Year 4 pupils can explore other properties of materials such as whether they are soluble (dissolve in water), whether they are attracted to magnets, or whether they conduct electricity.

Check your understanding

1. Can you define the term material?
2. Can you list some of the different materials found around us?

3. Can you explain the difference between the physical and chemical properties of a material?

4. Can you give the reasons why some objects are made from a particular material?

Key concept: how can the shape of materials be changed?

Associated vocabulary

bending, elastic limit, force, irreversible, mechanical changes, molecules, reversible, squashing, stiffness, stretching, twisting

---

Definitions

Mechanical changes are the changes that result from the application of a **force** to an object, such as **squashing**, **bending**, **twisting** or **stretching**. These forces can change the shape of the object. It may look different, but the actual material remains the same – that is, the material is still formed from the same type of **molecules** – and its mass remains the same. The **stiffness** of the material (the resistance of the material to elastic deformation) determines the extent of the change and whether the material is flexible or rigid. Mechanical changes are **reversible** if the material can return to its original shape. If the **elastic limit** is exceeded by the applied force, however, the change is said to be **irreversible**.

Examples

Modelling clay or putty are examples of common materials that can be squashed. Once the squashing force is removed, they will remain in their new shape as the material has been deformed. In contrast, if a rubber ball is squashed it can return to its original shape. A flexible plastic ruler will also return to its original shape once the force is removed.

In practice

Year 2

Draw an object on a balloon with a felt tip pen and show the children what you have drawn. Then ask the children to predict what will happen to the drawing when you blow up the balloon. Blow up the balloon and show them what happens. The object will increase in size and become deformed because it is stretched as the balloon expands. Then let the air out of the balloon and the object will go back to its original size and shape. Alternatively, run a competition to see who can make the longest 'worm' by stretching and squashing modelling clay. Talk about what has happened to the material after a force has been applied.

Check your understanding

1. Do you understand the term 'mechanical change'?

2. Can you give some examples of mechanical change?

3. Do you understand why some mechanical changes are reversible and some are not?

Key concept: what are solids, liquids and gases?

Associated vocabulary

colloids, gases, liquids, particles, physical properties, solids, states of matter, vibrate

---

Definitions

Materials or substances are often grouped into **solids**, **liquids** or **gases**. These are the three **states of matter** in which the particles behave in different ways (see Figure 5.1 below).

- In a solid, the **particles** are closely packed and arranged in a regular pattern. They **vibrate** about a fixed point, but there is no other movement. There is a strong bond between neighbouring particles. Solids have certain **physical properties**, which include being difficult to compress and having a fixed shape and volume. Solids can be heavy or light.

- In liquids, the particles are fairly closely packed together and are not arranged in a regular pattern. The particles are able to slide over one another and there is a weak bond between neighbouring particles. Liquids are difficult to compress; they do not have a fixed shape (they take up the shape of a container) and they can be heavy or light.

- In gases, the particles are widely spaced and are not arranged in a regular pattern. The particles are free to move in all directions and are not bonded to neighbouring particles. Gases can be compressed easily, they do not have a fixed shape or volume and are very light compared with solids and liquids.

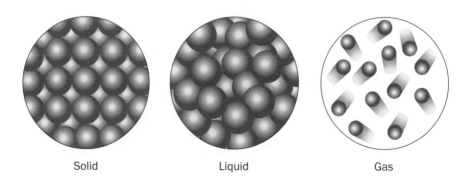

Solid   Liquid   Gas

Figure 5.1 *Arrangements of particles in solids, liquids and gases.*

Examples

Solid, liquid and gas are called the three states of matter. Wood is an example of a solid, as are powders such as flour or sugar. Water and petrol are examples of liquids. Air and steam are gases. Milk and toothpaste are common examples of **colloids**, in which small particles of one substance are evenly dispersed in another substance. Colloids are not covered in the national curriculum.

In practice

Year 4

Children can be asked to classify a range of materials (eg talcum powder, flour, orange juice, water, cheese or pasta) into solids, liquids or gases. It is best not to use colloidal materials such as toothpaste, shaving foam or mousse to avoid misconceptions.

An interesting extension activity (which does involve a colloid) is to mix cornflour with water and watch what happens. Place 450g of cornflour into a mixing bowl, add 475ml of water and mix together. Keep mixing until the cornflour and water are blended together to make a slime and then ask the children to try to punch the slime and then quickly withdraw their fist. They will find that this mixture instantly turns hard because, under the force of their punch, the water in the slime quickly flows away from the site of impact and leaves behind a very dense patch of cornflour particles in front of their fist. Ask them to then try scooping some of the slime into their hand and rolling it into a ball. If they keep applying pressure, the solid mixture will keep the shape of the ball. If they stop rubbing, however, it soon trickles back into the bowl as a liquid. The mixture of cornflour and water is a colloid and is not a liquid, solid or gas.

Check your understanding

1. Do you understand the differences between solids, liquids and gases?
2. Can you explain solids, liquids and gases using particle theory?
3. Can you give examples of the different states of matter?

Key concept: what is meant by changes of state?

Associated vocabulary

change of state, condensation, energy, evaporation, freeze, gas, liquid, melting, particles, particulate theory, physical changes, precipitation, reverse sublimation, reversible, solid, solidify, sublimation, substance, vibrate

Definitions

A **change of state** occurs when a **substance** changes from one state to another – for example, from a **solid** to a **liquid** or from a liquid to a **gas**. **Particulate theory** can be used to explain how changes of state between solids, liquids and gases – resulting from an increase or decrease in **energy** (usually from heating or cooling) – are interchangeable. When an object is heated, the motion of the **particles** increases as the particles gain energy. In contrast, if the material is cooled, the motion of the particles decreases as they lose energy. Eventually the material will **freeze** or **solidify**. Different materials have different melting and freezing points. The different changes of state are shown in Figure 5.2.

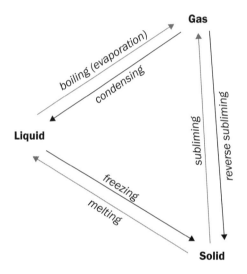

Figure 5.2 *Changes of state.*

Note that a solid can also change directly from a solid to a gas. This is known as **sublimation**. An example of a common compound that sublimes is carbon dioxide (dry ice), which is often used to preserve food by flash freezing.

These changes of state are **physical changes** and are **reversible** – that is, the material can go back to its original state through the processes of **melting, freezing, evaporation, condensation, sublimation** or **reverse sublimation** (see Figure 5.2).

Examples

In a solid such as butter, the strong attractions between the particles hold them together tightly, so even though they are vibrating about a fixed point, the structure is not disrupted. When butter is heated, the particles gain energy and start to **vibrate** faster. The structure of the material is initially weakened and the solid begins to expand. Further heating provides more energy until the particles eventually have enough energy to start to break free of their physical bonds, but they do not move further apart. Thus although the particles are still loosely connected, they are able to move around. At this point the solid is beginning to melt to form a liquid. Water is not a good example to use here because solid ice takes up more space than liquid water (ie water increases in volume when it freezes – this is why ice floats on the surface of a pond).

Some of the particles in a liquid have more energy than others. These more energetic particles may have sufficient energy to escape from the surface of the liquid as a gas. If heating continues, then eventually the particles are moving so rapidly that bubbles of gas form inside the liquid. As the temperature increases further, the rate of evaporation also increases. Evaporation can take place at room temperature, which is often well below the boiling point of the liquid. The actual boiling point is the temperature at which evaporation occurs in the centre of the liquid. The boiling point indicates how strongly the particles are held together in liquids. In liquids with high boiling points, the forces between the particles are stronger than in liquids with low boiling points.

As a gas is cooled, the particles start to move more slowly. As the temperature falls even further, the particles move more and more slowly. Eventually, the particles will not have enough energy to bounce off each other when they collide and they will cling together as a liquid. This is known as condensation.

The water cycle (see Figure 5.3) is a natural cycle and can be used to illustrate changes of state. The Sun heats up water in seas and lakes on the Earth's surface. This liquid water evaporates and enters the atmosphere as water vapour, which then rises and condenses to form clouds as the temperature decreases with the height above the surface. This water vapour eventually condenses into water droplets as the temperature continues to decrease with height. When the water droplets reach a certain size, they fall to the Earth as liquid rain or solid snow (**precipitation**), depending on the temperature. The cycle then begins again.

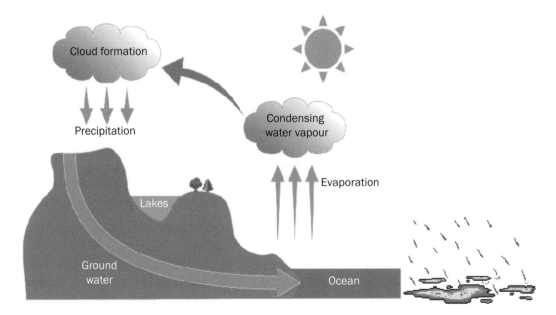

Figure 5.3 *Schematic diagram of the main processes in the water cycle.*

In practice

Year 4

Fill a balloon with water coloured with a food dye. Place the balloon in a freezer until the water freezes and you have an ice balloon. Talk to the children about the temperature at which the water froze. Peel the skin of the balloon away and place the balloon-shaped ice in a tank of water. Ask the children to predict what they think will happen to the ice balloon and the water. The ice balloon will start to melt and will become smaller until eventually it disappears. The water in the tank will take up the colour of the ice as it melts.

Reinforce the scientific terminology of some of the states of matter using labels and pictures. Ask the children to create a diagram of the water cycle. Ask them to identify the parts played by evaporation and condensation in the water cycle. Display their pictures in the classroom.

Check your understanding

1. Can you explain the changes of state with reference to particulate theory?

2. Can you describe and explain the processes involved in the changes from one state to another?

3. Do you know what is meant by a physical change and why it is reversible?

4. Are you confident in explaining how the water cycle works?

Key concept: what does dissolving mean?

Associated vocabulary

dissolving, evaporating, mixture, insoluble, saturation point, saturated solution, solid, soluble, solute, solvent, solution, substance, suspension

Definitions

Dissolving occurs when a **solid** mixes with a liquid and looks like it has disappeared, although it has, in fact, dispersed in the liquid to form a homogeneous **mixture** called a **solution**. The solid is called the **solute** and the liquid is called the **solvent**. The **substances** are mixed, but not combined chemically. The solid is said to have **dissolved** in the liquid.

Heat can help some substances to dissolve faster. Substances that dissolve in a liquid are said to be **soluble**. Substances that do not dissolve are said to be **insoluble**. There is a limit to the mass of solute that will dissolve in a given amount of solvent. A **saturated solution** is formed at this limit. Different solids will have different **saturation points**. The speed at which a solute dissolves in a liquid depends on the size of the individual pieces. Large pieces will take longer to dissolve than small pieces. The amount of a solid that can be dissolved in a liquid is increased if the temperature of the liquid is increased. Dissolution is an example of a physical change and is reversible.

Examples

A solution is formed when sugar is mixed with water. The sugar dissolves to form a transparent solution. Sugar is therefore soluble. Granules of sugar will dissolve faster than a whole sugar cube. Fine particles of salt that have been dissolved in water can be recovered by **evaporating** the water to leave the salt behind. This change is reversible as the solute can be recovered from the solvent.

Rice and pasta do not dissolve in water and are therefore insoluble. The undissolved solid particles of rice or pasta can be separated from the liquid using a sieve. The pasta is the residue. Filter paper is used to make filtered coffee. The filtrate (liquid coffee) passes through the filter paper and the residue (coffee grains) is retained on the filter.

If the solid will not dissolve in a liquid, the result may be a **suspension**. Muddy water is an example of a suspension. Muddy water can be separated into its component parts by simply allowing the sediment in the water to settle at the bottom of a bottle. The heavier sediments will settle at the bottom with the lighter sediments on top to form layers.

Dissolving and melting are often confused, but are different processes, as shown in the following table.

Dissolution	Melting
Can happen without heating	Heat is needed
Requires two or more substances	Only needs one substance
Usually involves a solid being added to a liquid	The substance remains pure
Cannot be reversed by cooling	Can be reversed by cooling
Involves two different kinds of particles mixing intimately	Involves the rearrangement of particles
	Involves a solid turning into a liquid

In practice

Year 5

Provide the children with a range of different types of sugar (eg caster sugar, granulated sugar, brown sugar and sugar cubes) and ask them to devise a fair test to determine which of these sugars will dissolve the fastest. More able children can be extended by asking them to investigate whether the temperature of the water affects the speed at which the sugars dissolve or to find out about the saturation points of the different types of sugars. The results can be recorded using line graphs, which links with the national curriculum requirement of Working Scientifically.

To liven things up, the children can be asked to find the original components of a wizard's mixture for a particular spell. Create a mixture made out of solutes with different particle sizes, such as salt, rice, sand, magnets, water and pebbles. The children can problem-solve and work out how to separate the components by sieving, filtering, evaporating and using magnets.

Check your understanding

1. Can you provide a concise definition of what dissolving is?

2. Can you explain why dissolving is a physical change and is reversible?

3. Can you define the terms solute, solvent, solution and saturation point?

4. Can you describe a variety of methods that can be used to separate a mixture?

Key concept: what is chemical change?

Associated vocabulary

atoms, burning, chemical change, compounds, elements, iron oxide, irreversible change, molecules, particles, rusting

Definitions

A **chemical change** occurs when a chemical reaction takes place in a material – for example, **burning** or **rusting.** The chemical bonds between the **particles** (**atoms** and **molecules**) of the substances (**elements** or **compounds)** are broken and new compounds are produced. The original materials are transformed into new materials. In primary schools, these changes are said to be **irreversible changes** – that is, the original material cannot be recovered.

Examples

Burning (combustion) is an example of a chemical change. When burned in oxygen, a fuel such as petrol produces carbon dioxide, water and a large amount of energy, which is used to drive the car. The original material (the petrol) cannot be recovered.

Rusting is another example of chemical change. Both water and oxygen are required for iron to rust. Rusting takes place in two stages. First, the atoms of iron react with the atoms of oxygen in the atmosphere to form **iron oxide**. The molecules of iron oxide then combine with molecules of water to form molecules of hydrated iron oxide or rust.

In practice

Year 6

Ask the children to work in pairs and place a tea-light into a tray of sand. Light the candle, adhering to all health and safety procedures (see *Be Safe in Science*, published by the Association for Science Education). Ask them to observe the candle burning and to make an annotated drawing of what they see. Ask them to note whether the changes they see are physical or chemical and prompt them to describe these changes.

Make popcorn with the children using a microwave oven. First show them the popping corn in the packet before it has been heated. Ask them to predict what will happen when it is heated in the microwave oven. After heating the popcorn, discuss what has happened to it and what type of change has taken place. Prompt your pupils to consider that they cannot get the popcorn back to the way it was in the packet.

Check your understanding

1. Do you understand, and can you explain, chemical change?
2. Can you provide some examples of chemical change?
3. Do you know why chemical change is described as irreversible in primary school?
4. Can you give an example of a chemical change that is reversible?
5. Can you explain the physical and chemical changes that are taking place when a candle burns?

6 Earth and space

What do you need to know to be able to teach this topic?

The national curriculum (DfE, 2013) places a statutory requirement on schools to teach pupils about seasonal changes and the Earth and space. It suggests pupils should be taught to:

- *observe changes across the four seasons*
- *observe and describe weather associated with the seasons and how day length varies*

(DfE, 2013: 143)

- *describe the movement of the Earth and other planets relative to the Sun in the solar system*
- *describe the movement of the Moon relative to the Earth*
- *describe the Sun, Earth and Moon as approximately spherical bodies*
- *use the idea of the Earth's rotation to explain day and night*

(DfE, 2013: 164).

SUBJECT KNOWLEDGE AUDIT

Use the following audit to identify the strengths and areas for development in your subject knowledge of this topic.

Using a scale of 1–4, rate your current level of competence:

1 = Excellent; 2 = Good; 3 = Satisfactory; 4 = Needs improvement.

	1	2	3	4
Explain how and why day length varies				
Describe the movement of the Earth and other planets relative to the Sun in the solar system				
Understand that the Sun is a star				
Know that there are eight planets in our solar system				
Describe the movement of the Moon relative to the Earth				
Understand that the Sun, Earth and Moon are approximately spherical bodies				
Understand the definition of a moon				
Explain that day and night are a result of the Earth's rotation and explain the apparent movement of the Sun across the sky				
Know how civilisation's ideas about the solar system have developed over time				

EARTH AND SPACE: CONCEPT MAP

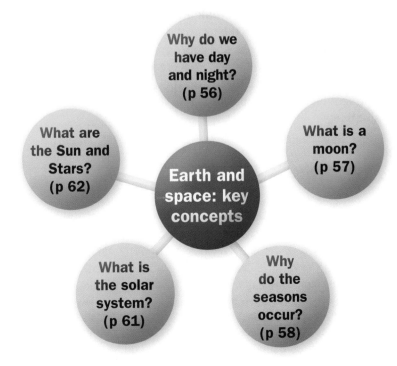

Key concept: why do we have day and night?

> ## Associated vocabulary
>
> axis, dawn, day, daybreak, dusk, gnomon, Greenwich Mean Time (GMT), midday, night, rotation, spins, summer solstice, sundial

Definitions

The Earth **spins** anti-clockwise on its **axis** once every 23 hours and 56 minutes. We round this up to 24 hours and say that a day is 24 hours long. This is the time it takes the Earth to complete one full **rotation** by spinning on its axis. Those parts of the Earth's surface that are exposed to sunlight experience **day**, while those parts that face away from the Sun experience **night**. All parts of the Earth's surface will therefore experience both night and day in a 24 hour cycle. The world is divided into 24 time zones. Each time zone is a region in which everyone uses the same time. If you look at a flat map, then the time zones to the right of the Greenwich Meridian, located at the Royal Greenwich Observatory in London, are ahead of Greenwich **Mean Time (GMT)**. Time zones to the left of the Greenwich Meridian are behind GMT.

Examples

The Sun rises in the east and sets in the west. The Sun appears to move across the sky, but it is important to remember that this is because the Earth is spinning on its axis, not because the Sun is moving across the sky.

We describe the rising of the Sun as **daybreak** and the time of day when our surroundings become lighter as **dawn**. **Dusk** refers to the time of day when the Sun is setting and daylight starts to fade. The time that the Sun rises and sets depends on the season. In winter, the Sun appears to be lower in the sky and will therefore set earlier. In contrast, the Sun appears to be higher in the sky in summer and will set later. Therefore we have fewer hours of daylight in the winter and longer nights; the opposite is true in the summer. The longest day occurs at the **summer solstice**.

In practice

Year 5

Ask the children to compare the times of day in different parts of the world. They can use internet links or direct communication such as telephone and email. For example, what time will it be in Mumbai or New York if it is 12 o'clock in London? Ask them to work out whether particular cities are ahead or behind GMT. For more able children, pose problems in which they catch a plane and fly from one city to another. Ask them to take into account the length of the flight and the time zones they are flying across to calculate their time of arrival.

Another useful activity is to look at the ways in which human beings have recorded the passage of time over the centuries using different devices such as water clocks. You could ask the children to carry out some research into Stonehenge and the various theories about why it was built; one of these theories is that the stones were used as an astronomical clock. In ancient times, people used sundials to mark the passage of hours and minutes. A **gnomon** is the name given to a **sundial** made from a vertical stick that casts a shadow on a sunny day. The length of the shadow is measured to determine the time.

Ask the children to construct a simple sundial or shadow clock. Once it has been calibrated, they can use it in the playground to show **midday** and the start and end of the school day. Instructions are given at the website listed at the end of this book.

Check your understanding

1. Do you know what causes day and night?

2. Can you explain the apparent movement of the Sun across the sky?

3. Can you explain why the number of hours of daylight varies between seasons?

4. Can you come up with your own practical activity to help children understand day and night?

Key concept: what is a moon?

Associated vocabulary

anti-clockwise, gravitational pull, lunar month, neap tides, orbits, satellite, secondary source, spring tides, tides, waning crescent, waning gibbous, waxing crescent, waxing gibbous

Definitions

A moon is a celestial body that **orbits** a planet. The planet Jupiter, for example, has four large moons and at least 46 smaller moons. The Earth has only one moon and it is often referred to as its only natural **satellite**. Moons themselves produce no light; we see our Moon because light from the Sun is reflected from its surface. It is therefore a **secondary** source of light. Our Moon is the second brightest object in the night sky. The Moon's surface is covered by craters and mountain ranges. The craters were formed by bombardment with rock debris during the early history of the solar system. The Moon has no atmosphere and there is no evidence of any living organisms on its surface.

Examples

Our Moon orbits the Earth in an **anti-clockwise** direction once every 27 days and seven hours. The Moon takes the same amount of time to rotate anti-clockwise on its own axis. Therefore one day on the Moon is equivalent to 27 days and seven hours on Earth. We always see the same side of the Moon because the time it takes to orbit the Earth is the same as the time it takes to make one complete rotation on its axis. The Moon is about a quarter of the size of the Earth and has one-sixth of the Earth's gravity.

A **lunar month** (29 days and 12 hours) is the average time between successive new or full moons. During this time, the illuminated part of the Moon has different shapes or phases. The first stage is a new Moon; we then see a **waxing crescent** as the illuminated part starts to get bigger. This is followed by the first quarter, where half of the Moon is illuminated, and then the **waxing gibbous** phase in which most of the Moon is illuminated. This is followed by a full Moon, when all of the Moon can be seen. The Moon then starts to wane and we see the **waning gibbous**, last quarter (half of the Moon is illuminated) and **waning crescent** phases. The whole cycle then begins again.

The Moon is the major cause of the Earth's **tides**, which occur as a result of the **gravitational pull** of the Moon on the oceans and, to a lesser extent, the pull of the Sun. As the Moon orbits the Earth, it pulls the Earth's oceans towards it. When the Sun and the Moon are both in line with the Earth their gravitational pulls reinforce each other and there are extra high tides known as **spring tides**. When the Sun and the Moon are at right angles to each other, their gravitational pulls act in opposition and smaller high tides, known as **neap tides**, occur.

In practice

Year 5

You could ask the children to keep a diary of the phases of the Moon. However, this may be impractical because, although the Moon rises and sets every day, it does so at different times. After the full phase, the Moon will not rise until after sunset and it rises later every night. When it gets too late, it is better to get up after sunrise and watch the Moon continue east. When it reaches the crescent phase, you may again need to get up before sunrise.

A better alternative might be to ask the children to make a lunar calendar for each day of the month, drawing the phase of the Moon for each day. Details of the phases of the Moon for particular days in a month can be easily accessed from the internet or a newspaper. Alternatively, they could make a flicker book to animate the different phases of the Moon.

Check your understanding

1.   Can you list the different phases of the Moon?
2.   Can you explain why we have different phases of the Moon?
3.   Can you explain why we always see the same face of the Moon?
4.   Can you describe why the Moon is responsible for the Earth's tides?
5.   Can you come up with your own practical activity to help children understand the phases of the Moon?

Key concept: why do the seasons occur?

Associated vocabulary

autumn, autumn equinox, axis, hemisphere, leap year, seasons, spring, spring equinox, summer, summer solstice, tilted, winter, winter solstice

Definitions

The **seasons** (**spring**, **summer**, **autumn** and **winter**) occur because the Earth's **axis** is **tilted** at 23.5° to the vertical as it rotates and orbits around the Sun. It takes the Earth 365.25 days to orbit around the Sun and we call this a year. Every four years we add the extra four-quarters together, which makes this year 366 days long – we call this a **leap year**.

When the northern **hemisphere** is tilted away from the Sun, it is winter in the northern hemisphere and summer in the southern hemisphere. The Sun is low in the sky during winter and its sunlight is spread over a large area of the Earth's surface. The heat energy from the Sun is therefore also dispersed and there is less heat in any one place. The **winter solstice** marks the shortest day and the longest night in the year.

When the northern hemisphere is tilted towards the Sun, it is summer in the northern hemisphere and winter in the southern hemisphere. The Sun is high in the sky and its rays are concentrated over a smaller area of the Earth's surface so there is more heat in any one place. The **summer solstice** marks the longest day of the year and the shortest night.

Day and night are approximately the same length at the **autumn** and **spring equinoxes**. After one complete year, the seasons are repeated as the Earth once more begins its orbit around the Sun (see Figure 6.1 below).

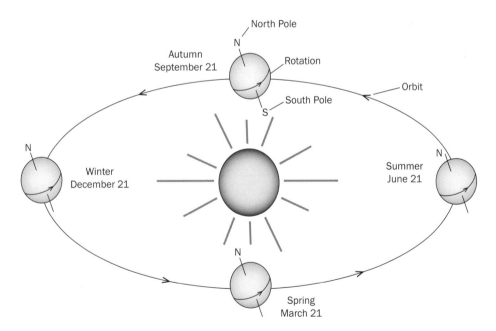

Figure 6.1 *Diagram showing why we have different seasons. In the northern hemisphere in summer, the North Pole is tilted towards the Sun. In winter in the northern hemisphere, the North Pole is tilted away from the Sun.*

Examples

Spring, summer, autumn and winter are the names of the four seasons. The weather changes during the seasons and we also see changes in the colour of the leaves on trees, in plant growth and in the behaviour of many animals. Humans wear different clothes as the temperature changes and eat different foods, as well as spending more or less of their leisure time outside.

- Spring sees the start of new life as the day length begins to increase and the weather becomes warmer. This is sometimes accompanied by increased rainfall. Seeds germinate and take root, plants start to grow and the leaves grow back on the trees. Animals come out of hibernation and those that have migrated to warmer climates return.

- As we approach summer, the temperature increases to the hottest of the year. Daylight hours are long and humans wear less clothing and eat colder foods.

- As autumn approaches, the day length begins to shorten. Temperatures start to cool and leaves change colour and fall from deciduous trees. Animals prepare for the colder weather by returning to countries with warmer climates or by storing food for the winter.

- Winter sees shorter hours of daylight and colder temperatures. Humans wear warmer clothing and eat hot food to stay warm.

In practice

Year 1

Make collages with the children using items that they have found outside during a walk in the local park or school grounds. For example, use leaves, twigs and dead flowers. Ask them to talk about the colours of the different seasons and the weather associated with spring, summer, autumn and winter. Ask them which animals can be seen during the different seasons and where these animals might be in other seasons if they are no longer visible. Alternatively, ask them to sequence the events that occur in their lives during a single year using a time line. Ask them to consider what they eat, wear and do during the different seasons and give reasons why this may be so. Ask them to think about the number of hours of daylight during the year and how this influences what they do after the school day finishes.

Check your understanding

1. Can you explain what causes the seasons?

2. Do you know why we have leap years?

3. Do you know what happens during the winter and summer solstices?

4. Do you know what the autumn and spring equinoxes are?

5. Can you come up with your own practical activity to help children understand why seasons occur?

Key concept: what is the solar system?

Associated vocabulary

asteroids, Alhazen, comets, Copernicus, dwarf planet, Earth, elliptical orbits, geocentric, gravitational pull, heliocentric, inner planets, Jupiter, Mars, Mercury, meteors, meteorites, Neptune, orbit, outer planets, planet, Pluto, Ptolemy, Saturn, solar nebula, solar system, spherical, Sun, Uranus, Venus

Definitions

The **solar system** was formed about 4.6 billion years ago by the gravitational collapse of a massive cloud called a **solar nebula**. The solar system consists of the **Sun** and the objects that **orbit** around it. A **planet** is a body that orbits the **Sun**. Planets are bodies that are large enough for their own gravity to have made them roughly **spherical** and which have cleared their orbit of other planets. Planets do not emit their own light and are seen because light from the Sun is reflected from their surfaces. Most of the planets in our solar system are orbited by moons. **Asteroids** are small rocky or metallic bodies that orbit the Sun and are concentrated in the asteroid belt between the planets **Mars** and **Jupiter**. They vary in size from a few metres in diameter to more than 1000m across.

Comets are small bodies that orbit the Sun in large elliptical orbits. They are 'dirty snowballs' made of ice and dust and only become visible from the Earth when they approach the Sun. The temperature rises as the comet moves closer to the Sun and its ice begins to melt and evaporate to form water vapour, releasing dust as it does so. Comets can be observed in the night sky trailing long tails of gas and dust. The most famous is Halley's comet, which was depicted in the Bayeux tapestry.

When particles of dust and rock fragments from space enter the Earth's atmosphere and burn up, they become shooting stars or **meteors**. If they do not burn up completely, they may fall to Earth as rock fragments called **meteorites**. Meteorites sometimes create huge craters when they hit the Earth's surface at high speeds – for example, Meteor Crater in Arizona is more than 1.5km in diameter.

Examples

All of the planets in the solar system move around the Sun in the same direction in **elliptical orbits**. The four **inner planets** (**Mercury**, **Venus**, **Earth** and **Mars**) are closest to the Sun. They are rocky planets with metallic cores. The giant **outer planets** (**Jupiter**, **Saturn**, **Uranus** and **Neptune**) are further away from the Sun. These planets are composed mainly of gases such as hydrogen and helium and have smaller rocky cores. **Pluto** was reclassified as a **dwarf planet** in 2006 because its elliptical orbit overlapped with that of Neptune. **Pluto**'s orbit is highly inclined, travelling at an angle of 17 degrees.

All the planets in the solar system are kept in orbit around the Sun by the Sun's **gravitational pull**; the Sun contains 99.8 per cent of the mass of the solar system. This is known as the **heliocentric** view of the solar system, in which the Earth and other planets revolve around a relatively stationary Sun at the centre. The Ancient Greeks, however, believed in a **geocentric model** in which the Earth was at the centre of the universe and all other objects orbited around it.

In practice

Year 5

Ask the children to carry out some research into the geocentric model of the solar system developed by philosophers such as **Ptolemy** in Ancient Greece. Ask them to compare this model with the heliocentric model accepted today. The children could perhaps even have a debate and put forward and consider both the heliocentric and geocentric points of view. Using books or internet sources, they could link this research with writing a biography of **Alhazen**, a Persian astronomer who made significant contributions to astronomy in the eleventh century.

Children could make models of the solar system in the form of an orrery using a variety of balls and spheres of different sizes painted in different colours. Alternatively, they could make papier mâché or plaster of Paris models of the planets. They could carry out some research on each of the planets, perhaps creating a table to compare their colour, size and distance from the Sun.

Safety note: remember to warn pupils of the dangers of looking at the Sun directly even when wearing dark glasses.

Check your understanding

1. Can you provide a concise definition of a planet?
2. Can you name all the planets in the solar system?
3. Can you explain how the solar system was created?
4. Can you come up with your own practical activity to help children understand the orbit of the planets around the Sun?

Key concept: what are the Sun and stars?

Associated vocabulary

Andromeda galaxy, asterisms, black hole, celestial sphere, constellations, galaxies, helium, hydrogen, Local Group, Milky Way, neutron star, planetary nebula, red giant, red supergiant, Sirius, supernova, white dwarf

Definitions

Stars are huge luminous spheres composed largely of plasma (charged ions) and held together by strong gravitational forces. Stars produce heat, visible light and other forms of electromagnetic radiation such as X-rays and ultraviolet radiation. The nearest star to Earth is the Sun, which provides us with both heat and light. Other stars are visible from the Earth during the hours of darkness; they look like luminous point sources of light because they are such a long way away from us. The most prominent stars were grouped into **constellations** in historical times (eg Orion and the Great Bear) and the brightest stars were given names – for example, **Sirius**, the brightest star in the night sky, is also known as the Dog Star.

Our Sun is a middle-aged star and is about 4.5 billion years old. It is expected to remain stable for another four billion years. All stars have a life cycle and we can tell their temperature and age by their brightness and colour (see Figure 6.2 below). Stars are created in vast, rotating clouds of interstellar gas and dust, which, when they reach a certain critical state, collapse and contract as a result of gravitational forces. The central region of condensed matter begins to heat up and will eventually reach temperatures high enough for **hydrogen** nuclei to fuse and form **helium** nuclei. The star then begins to release energy in the form of electromagnetic radiation and starts to shine. In stars of average mass, like our Sun, the outer layers of the star will eventually expand, cool and shine less brightly over a time period of billions of years. As this occurs, the familiar yellow colour of our Sun will change and our star will become a **red giant**. When all the helium in its core has been used up, the outer layers of the Sun will drift away from the core to form a gaseous shell called a **planetary nebula.** The remaining core is now in the final stages of its existence and is known as a **white dwarf**. The Sun will eventually cool and dim further and will end its life as a small, dense, cold sphere about the size of the Earth.

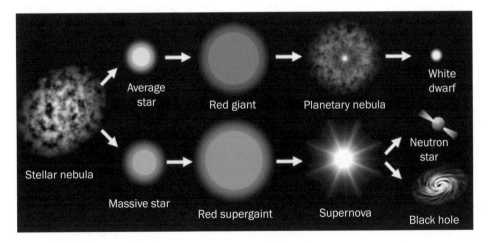

Figure 6.2 *The life cycles of stars. Medium-sized stars such as our Sun end their lives as white dwarfs, whereas massive stars explode dramatically as supernovas. Depending on the initial size of the star, the remnant cores of supernovas become either neutron stars or black holes.*

In contrast, more massive stars evolve into **red supergiants**. The death of these massive stars is very dramatic. After all their fuel has been used up, their cores suddenly collapse under gravity over a matter of days and this causes an enormous explosion called a **supernova**. During this explosion, the shock wave blows off the outer layers of the star into the interstellar medium. If the surviving core is between one and a half and three solar masses, it contracts to become a tiny, very dense **neutron star**. However, if the core is much greater than three solar masses, it contracts to become a **black hole**.

Examples

The Earth orbits the Sun at a distance of 150,000,000km. You could line up more than 100 Earths across its diameter and fit 1.3 million Earths into its volume. It is composed of 74 per cent hydrogen, 25 per cent helium and 1 per cent heavier elements. The temperature of the surface of the Sun is about 5500°C, but temperatures in the core, where hydrogen nuclei fuse to form helium nuclei, are close to 15 million degrees. The Sun is the only object in the solar system that produces its own heat.

Of the many thousands of stars visible in the night sky, only a few hundred have been given proper names. Instead, stars are grouped into named patterns called **asterisms**. A constellation is now defined as one of 88 specific areas of the **celestial sphere**. These areas cover the whole of the night sky and any point in the sky can be assigned to a constellation. This gives us a way to unambiguously describe the position of any celestial object such as a star or planet.

Galaxies are vast systems of stars, the remnants of stars and interstellar gas and dust bound together by gravity. The universe contains more than 200 billion galaxies, most of which contain more than 100 billion stars. Our own galaxy is a spiral galaxy and can be seen as a band of stars running across the night sky – this band is known as the **Milky Way**. The **Andromeda galaxy** is the nearest galaxy to us, but light from this galaxy still takes 2.5 million years to reach us. Galaxies occur in clusters. Our own galaxy is part of a cluster known as the **Local Group**.

In practice

Year 5

Ask the children to draw the life cycle of a star, first for stars of a similar mass to our Sun and then for massive stars one and a half to three times the mass of the Sun. Ask them to sequence the different stages and use the correct scientific terminology, such as red giant or supernova. Encourage them to use both pictures and writing to explain the different stages. The NASA website will provide them with useful information to complete the task.

Ask the children to find out about the different constellations in the night sky. Encourage them to use a telescope or binoculars and a sky map to view the night sky and identify some of the more famous examples, such as Orion or the Plough. Prompt them to compare the different constellations found in the northern and southern hemispheres. Ask them to find out how ancient mariners used the constellations and stars to help them navigate when at sea. If possible, visit a planetarium.

Check your understanding

1.   Can you define a star?

2.   Can you describe the life cycle of a star using scientific terminology such as red giant, supernova or neutron star?

3.   Can you provide a concise definition of what a galaxy is and talk about some well-known galaxies such as the Milky Way?

4.   Can you give a range of examples to children of the constellations and stars found in the night sky?

7 Rocks

What do you need to know to be able to teach this topic?

The national curriculum (DfE, 2013) places a statutory requirement on schools to teach pupils about rocks and soils. It suggests pupils should be taught to:

- *compare and group together different kinds of rocks on the basis of their appearance and simple physical properties*

- *describe in simple terms how fossils are formed when things that have lived are trapped in rocks*

- *recognise that soils are made from rocks and organic matter*

(DfE, 2013: 158).

SUBJECT KNOWLEDGE AUDIT

Use the following audit to identify the strengths and areas for development in your subject knowledge of this topic.

Using a scale of 1–4, rate your current level of competence:

1 = Excellent; 2 = Good; 3 = Satisfactory; 4 = Needs improvement.

	1	2	3	4
Compare and group different kinds of rocks on the basis of their appearance, origin and simple physical properties				
Define the main groups of rocks (metamorphic, sedimentary and igneous), including details of their origin, appearance and physical properties				
Describe how fossils are formed				
Name a variety of fossil types				
Assign habitats to a range of fossils				
Describe the processes of weathering and erosion				
Name a variety of soil types and their origins				
Explain how soils are made from rocks and organic matter				

ROCKS: CONCEPT MAP

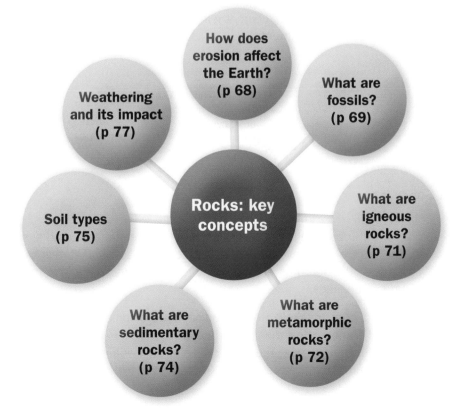

Key concept: how does erosion affect the Earth?

> ## Associated vocabulary
>
> deposits, glaciers, ice, moraine, rocks, sediments, transporting, water, waves, wind

Definitions

Erosion is the process whereby **rocks** and other **deposits** on the Earth's surface are worn away by the action of natural agents such as **wind**, **water** and **ice**. Erosion has formed many features on the Earth's surface, such as valleys, mountains and coastlines. No rock is hard enough to resist the action of erosion. The Grand Canyon in Arizona, for example, has been formed by the erosion of rocks by the Colorado River. Humans may increase the rate of erosion through activities such as farming, tree-felling and urban development. Trees and plants hold soils in place, but when they are cut down, the soil may be washed or blown away more easily. The word erosion is derived from the Latin word *erosionem*, which means gnawing away.

Examples

Erosion can be gradual or may occur quickly depending on the forces that cause it. Water is the major agent of erosion on Earth and generally produces rapid erosion. Rivers break up rocks and boulders on the river bed and carry them downstream (see Figure 7.1). The transported materials are known as **sediments**.

The bedload (sand and stones) wears away the river bed as the water flows

Figure 7.1 *Erosion in a river.*

Another example of water erosion is the **waves** crashing on the shoreline and against cliffs at the seaside. The force of the waves may alter the coastline and sometimes leads to the formation of caves and other features. Waves pound rocks into pebbles and reduce pebbles into the sand found on beaches.

Wind is the main type of erosion in arid areas. Wind causes erosion by moving loose particles of sand and dust and **transporting** them from one place to another. The wind can sometimes blow sand into towering dunes. The sand dunes in the Badain Jaran area of the Gobi Desert in China, for example, are more than 400m high. Wind-blown sand is also blasted against rocks and slowly wears away softer rocks and polishes rocks and cliffs until they are smooth.

Glaciers move much more slowly than liquid water. Despite this, they can carve out huge valleys and mountains. Glaciers can move large boulders and tiny grains of sand. As they are moved, these rocks scrape against the ground below, wearing it away. There have been a number of periods during the last 2.6 million years when the Earth's temperature was much lower than today. This resulted in several so-called 'ice ages' in which the northern hemisphere was covered by vast glaciers. These glaciers carved many of the characteristic features seen today in the hills of Scotland and the English Lake District, and also carved the deep inlets or fjords seen along the coast of Scandinavia. Glaciers are still present today in some mountain ranges, such as the Alps and the Himalayas. The rock debris deposited by glaciers is known as **moraine**.

In practice

Year 3

To help children to understand the processes of erosion, ask them to investigate what happens when rocks are rubbed together. Use rocks of different hardness so that they can appreciate how softer rocks such as chalk will erode more quickly than a harder rock such as basalt.

Ask children to explore what changes occur when rocks are immersed in water. Try holding a sugar cube or ice cube under a slowly dripping tap and record what happens to its shape. This will give them an appreciation of the power of water. Ask them to locate the Grand Canyon on a map of the USA and ask how it might have formed. Ask them to look carefully at the steep sides of the canyon and explain how the River Colorado has cut a channel through the layers of rock over millions of years – and continues to do so today.

Check your understanding

1. Can you provide a concise definition of erosion?
2. Can you explain the different types of erosion?
3. Can you provide examples of each type of erosion?
4. Can you come up with your own practical activity to help children understand erosion?

Key concept: what are fossils?

Associated vocabulary

ammonites, dinosaurs, *Homo erectus*, palaeontologists, trilobites

Definitions

Fossils are the remains, or traces, of ancient plants or animals that have been preserved within a rock. The word fossil derives from the Latin *fossilis*, meaning 'dug up'. Geologists can now tell the age of a fossil through a variety of dating techniques and this allows them to sequence their finds to help unravel our evolutionary history. Fossils are formed when either the traces of organisms or the actual living or dead organism itself become buried in sand, soil or mud. These sediments are compressed over time by the weight of sediments that form above them. Chemicals or minerals often replace the original structure, changing its chemical composition and preserving it, or by making a cast of the original shape.

Examples

Fossils provide us with rich evidence of the variety of life forms that once inhabited the Earth. Unfortunately, the fossil record is incomplete, as particular conditions have to be met for preservation. Soft body tissues are not preserved in this way, so most body fossils are hard bones or teeth. Despite the incomplete record, fossils have given us an insight into the evolution of many species. The scientists who study fossils are called **palaeontologists**.

Body fossils that have been studied in detail include **trilobites**, **ammonites**, the preserved skeletons of **dinosaurs** (eg *Triceratops*) and the skeletons and teeth of early humans (eg ***Homo erectus***). Ancient creatures such as trilobites lived deep in the ocean and looked like modern day woodlice. Ammonites lived in ribbed, spiral-shaped shells and are related to our modern day octopus, squid, cuttlefish and nautilus. Fossils provide insights into how the climate and surface conditions of the Earth have changed over geological time. Trace fossils are traces of the activities of ancient creatures. They include the burrows left by marine bivalves and footprints left on an originally soft surface such as a muddy shoreline.

In practice

Year 3

Provide pupils with a range of fossils and a magnifying glass and ask them to draw and describe what they see. Encourage pupils to explain whether this creature was once alive and, if so, why? Ask the children to think about creatures living today and whether there are any similarities between the fossils and modern plants or animals. This will allow them to draw parallels between the present and the past by making links about how these organisms lived. Allow pupils to access secondary sources such as books and the internet to research the creatures they are studying. You could ask them to produce a fact-file linked to a particular organism to consolidate their understanding.

To help pupils understand how fossils are created, you can ask them to create their own 'fossils'. Provide the children with some large seashells and some modelling clay. Ask the children to roll the clay out into a rectangle about 2cm thick with a 2cm high rim around its edge. Ask the children to imagine that the creature which lived in the shell has died and that the shell has fallen onto an ancient seafloor with the concave surface upwards. Ask the children to press the shell into the clay to create a mould. This represents the weight of other layers of sediment pressing down on this shell over long periods of geological time. Then remove the shell from the clay and pour some plaster of Paris into the mould you have created. Tell the children that this represent the sediments that have covered the creature up and that these soft sediments will eventually turn into harder rocks. Once the plaster has set, the children can peel the clay off the plaster cast and see that the shape and texture of the shell are now preserved.

Safety note: remember to keep pupils safe by ensuring they wear goggles and gloves.

Check your understanding

1. Can you provide a concise definition of what a fossil is?

2. Can you name a range of fossils and the animals they are derived from?

3. Can you explain how fossils are created as a result of geological processes?

4. Can you come up with your own practical activity to help children understand fossils?

Key concept: what are igneous rocks?

Associated vocabulary

basalt, crust, crystalline, extrusive, granite, igneous rocks, intrusive, lava, magma, mantle, pumice, plutons, volcanic, volcanoes

Definitions

Igneous rocks are formed when molten rock (**magma**) cools and solidifies. **Intrusive** igneous rocks are formed when the magma solidifies beneath the Earth's surface. These igneous rocks generally cool down slowly and may form large bodies called **plutons**. **Extrusive** igneous rocks are formed on the surface of the Earth when magma is extruded through **volcanoes** or fissures as hot **lava**. Igneous rocks are **crystalline** and the size of the crystals depends on how fast the magma cooled. Large crystals indicate that the magma cooled slowly underground. **Volcanic** rocks have much smaller crystals as they cooled quickly when they were extruded onto the Earth's surface.

Examples

Examples of igneous rocks include **granite, pumice** and **basalt**. Granite is formed deep in the Earth's **crust** by the partial melting of other rocks. Good examples of granite are seen in Devon where they make up the high, erosion-resistant tors found on Dartmoor. Pumice is a grey, fine-grained volcanic rock that contains many air holes and fine, glass-like filaments. This makes pumice very light and some samples can float on water. Pumice is formed from the solidification of a gas-rich volcanic froth. Basalt is a dark-coloured, fine-grained rock formed by partial melting of the Earth's **mantle**. Basalt covers about 70 per cent of the Earth's surface. The upper layers of the ocean floors are made of basalt.

In practice

Year 3

Provide children with a variety of igneous rocks, such as granite and pumice, and a hand lens. Ask them to look carefully at these rocks and to describe and draw what they see. Encourage the children to identity the crystalline features of the granite and the melted, frothy, glass-like features of the pumice. Encourage them to consider the origins of these rocks and guide them to realise that they have been formed by melting caused by processes within the Earth. You can then suggest that they could make their own 'granite' by cooking and using ingredients to represent its constituent parts. Using a basic cake mixture, add chopped cherries, currants and raisins to represent the crystals that make up this rock and then bake this mixture. When the children slice open their cake they will be able to see a similar structure to granite and realise how the process of heating and cooling has made this item solid.

Check your understanding

1.   Can you provide a concise definition of an igneous rock?

2.   Can you explain how Earth processes have led to the formation of these rocks?

3.   Can you give a range of examples of the main types of igneous rocks?

4.   Can you come up with your own practical activity to help children understand about igneous rocks?

Key concept: what are metamorphic rocks?

Associated vocabulary

gneiss, marble, metamorphic rocks, schist, slate

Definitions

Metamorphic rocks are formed from igneous or sedimentary rocks that have been changed or 'metamorphosed' by the effects of heat and/or pressure deep within the Earth. Metamorphic rocks are crystalline and often have textures showing banding or folding. The type of metamorphic rock formed depends on how much pressure and heat the rock was subjected to and for how long.

Examples

There is a huge variety of metamorphic rocks. **Marble** is formed when limestone is metamorphosed and is often used for building and carving statues because it is very hard and can be polished. One famous example is Michelangelo's statue of David. Sedimentary rocks such as mudstones and shale are metamorphosed into **slate**. Slate is a very hard rock with a dull grey–blue lustre and a strong cleavage, which makes it ideal to be split and used as roofing material. **Schists** and **gneiss** are metamorphic rocks that were formed at very high temperatures and pressures. The minerals in these rocks are organised into layers or bands, with each layer representing a different composition. The rocks often show folded structures that were formed when the rocks were squeezed under high pressure. Gneiss is often used for gravestones or as a building stone. It is predominately found in ancient or modern mountain ranges, such as in north-west Scotland or the European Alps.

In practice

Year 3

Using images or samples of metamorphic rocks such as schists and slates, encourage the children to notice the crystalline and banded nature of these rocks. Ask the children to consider how these rocks might have formed. Using images of folds, encourage the pupils to realise that Earth processes must have squeezed and heated these rocks so that they were deformed and changed over geological time. Suggest to the children that, because these changes took place deep in the Earth, it is difficult to mimic them. However, you can give them an insight into such processes on a small scale using the following activity.

Using a large pencil sharpener, ask the children to sharpen four coloured crayons to create large shavings. Then ask the children to slightly flatten the shavings and place them in coloured layers in a pile in the centre of a 5cm square piece of aluminium foil. Ask the children to fold up the sides of the aluminium foil to make a boat-like structure. You should then, while warning the pupils to be careful, pour boiling water into a bowl and ask the children to place their boat on the hot water for 20 to 25 seconds. This should be enough time for the shavings to start to melt. Quickly lift the boat out of the water and fold the foil in half so that you can press the encased shavings flat. Once the foil is cool, ask the children to open it and have a look at what they have created. They will see a similar banding and folding to the rocks they have just examined.

Check your understanding

1. Can you explain how Earth processes have led to the formation of these rocks?

2. Can you provide a concise definition of what a metamorphic rock is?

3. Can you give a range of examples to children of the main types of metamorphic rocks and where they might be found?

4. Can you come up with your own practical activity to help children understand metamorphic rocks?

Key concept: what are sedimentary rocks?

Associated vocabulary

bedding, coal, chalk, conglomerates, fossils, limestone, sandstone, sedimentary rocks

---

Definitions

A **sedimentary rock** is formed when sediments originating from eroded rocks or the skeletal remains of plants or animals are deposited at the bottom of a river, lake, sea or ocean. These sediments are compressed over time by the weight of later sediments to form sedimentary rocks.

Sedimentary rocks often contain **fossils** of the ancient creatures that used to live in the environment in which the rocks formed. Many sedimentary rocks show distinct **bedding**, with the individual beds representing the original layers of sediment.

Examples

The sedimentary rocks found in the UK include **sandstones** formed by the deposition of sediments derived from the erosion of earlier rocks by rivers, or from ancient sand dunes formed when the local climate was more arid than today. **Conglomerates** contain fragments of large pebbles in a fine-grained matrix and were deposited for example by fast-flowing water. **Limestones** contain the remains of living creatures such as corals and bivalves that lived in warm, shallow seas and **chalk** is a very soft, porous, fine-grained rock composed of the mainly microscopic skeletal remains of tiny creatures that inhabited these ancient seas. **Coal** was formed from plant remains deposited in swampy conditions, as evidenced by the small fragments of ferns that can be found within it.

When studying these rocks, it is important to help pupils consider how these rocks give clues about the ancient environments in which they were formed. This allows the children to consider the dynamic nature of the Earth and how its landscape and climate are constantly changing.

In practice

Year 3

By providing pupils with a range of sedimentary rocks and a hand lens, you can encourage them to look at the composition of these rocks. Encourage them to start to draw modern day parallels with what they can see, such as shells and sand grains, and ask them to consider what type of environment these rocks might now be found in. In this way you can guide pupils to discover the origins of these rocks.

You can then suggest to the children that they could make their own 'conglomerate' using a simple cooking activity. Using a large mixing bowl, add plain biscuits that have been broken up by the children, along with raisins and sultanas. The broken biscuits symbolise the erosion of rocks, while the raisins and sultanas represent the variety of different rock types found in a conglomerate. Next, over a large bowl of warm water, use a mixing bowl to melt several bars of milk chocolate. When this turns into a liquid, ask the children to pour this 'river' of chocolate over the biscuits, raisins and sultanas. Encourage the children to see how the river of chocolate carries the sediments within it. You could ask them to stir the mixture to represent the eddies and currents within the river. Pour the mixture into a deep medium-sized tin and allow it to solidify. When you remove the mixture from the tin, you can slice it into squares and allow the pupils to observe the conglomerate-like nature of their creation.

Check your understanding

1. Can you provide a concise definition of what a sedimentary rock is?

2. Can you explain how Earth processes have led to the formation of these rocks?

3. Can you give a range of examples of the main type of sedimentary rocks and where they might be found?

4. Can you come up with your own practical activity to help children understand sedimentary rocks?

Key concept: soil types

Associated vocabulary

acidic, alkaline, bedrock, clay, climate, organic matter, nutrients, peat, sand, sediments, silt, soils, subsoil, topsoil, weathered

Definitions

Soils are made from **weathered** rocks and **organic matter**. They include weathered particles of the original bedrock, decaying and decayed organic matter, air, and water. The Earth's surface has been weathered over millions of years and these particles and **sediments** have led to the formation of different types of soil. The nature of the soil in any area will depend on the **bedrock**, the local **climate**, the topography and the length of time the bedrock has been exposed to weathering. Soil is capable of retaining water and it provides **nutrients** for plants and supports a range of different organisms, from microscopic bacteria to earthworms. The word soil originates from the Latin *solium*, a seat, but is often confused with the Latin word *solum*, meaning the ground.

Examples

There are different types of soils. Clay soils are heavy, high in **nutrients** and are wet and cold in winter and baked dry in summer. Sandy soils are light, dry, warm, low in nutrients and often **acidic.** Silty soils are fertile, light, moisture-retentive and easily compacted. Loams are mixtures of **clay**, **sand** and **silt** that avoid the extremes of each type. **Peat** soils are very high in organic matter and moisture. Chalky soils are very **alkaline** and are usually light.

Soil is made up of different layers. The top layer, often called the **topsoil**, is usually the darkest and is where plants and other organisms live. The level below this is called the **subsoil** and contains larger stones, clay and gravel. Below the subsoil is solid bedrock.

In practice

Year 3

To help children understand the differences between soils, ask them to bring in soils from their garden in polythene bags. Provide them with a magnifying glass and ask them to describe the similarities and differences between the soils. Help them to understand terms such as 'loam' or 'clay' by first removing any small stones or other non-soil items that may be present, either by hand or by sieving. Ask the children to take a small amount of soil and roll it into a ball in their hands. If the soil seems too dry, add a small amount of water to wet it slightly. Ask them to describe what it looks like and whether it feels sticky or a bit gritty. Ask them to try to roll the soil ball out into a sausage and see how thin they can make it before it breaks up. If they have managed to make a sausage, then ask them whether they can bend it into a horseshoe shape, or whether it cracks apart. Clay soils can be manipulated in this way, but a sandy soil will fall apart.

Children can be helped to understand the composition of soil and to appreciate the variety of particle sizes and the type of organic matter by carrying out the following activity. You will need a jar, soil, water and a sieve. Sieve the soil to remove any large particles and break up any big clumps. Add enough soil to fill the bottom third of the jar. Top it up to about three-quarters full with water. Screw the lid on tightly and shake vigorously for two or three minutes, making sure that, when you stop, all the soil has been mixed up with the water. Place the jar somewhere where it will not be disturbed for a few days and wait until the water clears. You will see that the mixture settles into different layers, with the lightest particles at the top and the heaviest at the bottom.

Safety note: remind the children that they need to work safely and wash their hands if they are handling soil.

Check your understanding

1. Can you explain how soil is formed?

2. Can you describe the different types of soil and their characteristics?

3. Can you explain the function of mini-beasts such as worms in soils?

4. Can you come up with your own practical activity to help children understand soils?

Key concept: weathering and its impact

Associated vocabulary

biological weathering, chemical weathering, decay, decomposition, freeze–thaw, ice, physical weathering, rain, soil, waves, weathering, wind

Definitions

Weathering is the gradual process by which rocks are slowly worn away. There is no movement associated with weathering and thus it should not be confused with erosion, which involves the movement and transport of rocks and minerals by water, ice, wind and gravity.

Weathering is often classified into three types: **physical weathering**, **chemical weathering** and **biological weathering**. The effects of weathering range from a change in the colour of a rock to the complete breakdown of minerals into clay. Some of the most beautiful rocks and land formations seen on Earth owe their shapes to the forces of weathering. The materials left over after the rock has broken down help to create **soil.** The mineral content of the soil is thus determined by the parent material.

Examples

Physical weathering is caused by physical changes, such as changes in temperature, and the effects of **wind**, **rain**, **ice** and **waves**. A rock will expand when it is heated and will contract when it becomes colder. If this happens many times, cracks appear and pieces of rock fall away. The wind can also blow tiny grains of sand against a rock, which will eventually wear the rock away. Ice can also break rocks. If water gets into a crack in a rock and then freezes, it expands and pushes the crack further apart. When the ice later melts, water can enter further into the crack. When the rock freezes again, it expands and makes the crack even bigger. This **freeze–thaw** process continues until eventually the rock will break.

Chemical weathering is a process of **decay** or **decomposition**. During chemical weathering, chemical reactions break down the minerals in a rock and, as a result, the rock may break into smaller pieces. Chemical weathering is most rapid in hot and humid climates, but is even present in the Arctic. Chemical weathering may involve rainwater that has been acidified by the absorption of carbon dioxide or pollutants.

Biological weathering is caused by the effects of living organisms such as plants and animals. It is often caused by chemicals released by the living plant or animal, or during the decay of their remains.

In practice

Year 3

Ask the children to draw examples of weathering in the environment – for example, cracked pavements, monuments or gravestones. Provide them with a magnifying glass so that they can observe the effects closely. Encourage them to take photographs of rocks that are being weathered in the natural environment, such as cracks in rocks, plants growing in rocks, or rock falls under cliffs, and try to explain what is happening. Ask them to test and record the effects of shaking sugar cubes and gravel together in a jar.

A simple way of demonstrating that water expands as it freezes is by pouring water into a cup and marking the water level, then placing the cup in a freezer. Mark the level of the water once it has frozen into ice. Ask the children to compare the two marks.

Check your understanding

1. Can you define the term weathering and do you understand the difference between weathering and erosion?

2. Can you describe the different types of weathering?

3. Can you provide examples of the different types of weathering seen in the environment?

4. Can you come up with your own practical activity to help children understand weathering?

8 Light

What do you need to know to be able to teach this topic?

The national curriculum (DfE, 2013) places a statutory requirement on schools to teach pupils about light. It suggests that pupils in lower Key Stage 2 should be taught to:

- *recognise that they need light in order to see things and that dark is the absence of light*

- *notice that light is reflected from surfaces*

- *recognise that light from the Sun can be dangerous and that there are ways to protect their eyes*

- *recognise that shadows are formed when the light from a light source is blocked by a solid object*

- *find patterns in the way that the size of shadows change*

(DfE, 2013: 159).

In upper Key Stage 2 pupils should:

- *use the idea that light travels in straight lines to explain that objects are seen because they give out or reflect light into the eye*

- *explain that we see things because light travels from light sources to our eyes or from light sources to objects and then to our eyes*

- *use the idea that light travels in straight lines to explain why shadows have the same shape as the objects that cast them.*

(DfE, 2013: 174).

SUBJECT KNOWLEDGE AUDIT

Use the following audit to identify the strengths and areas for development in your subject knowledge of this topic.

Using a scale of 1–4, rate your current level of competence:

1 = Excellent; 2 = Good; 3 = Satisfactory; 4 = Needs improvement.

	1	2	3	4
Compare and group different materials depending on whether they are transparent, translucent or opaque				
Describe both primary and secondary sources of light				
Explain how light travels				
Explain how a shadow is formed				
Name the parts of a human eye				
Describe the dangers associated with light				
Explain how a rainbow is formed				

LIGHT: CONCEPT MAP

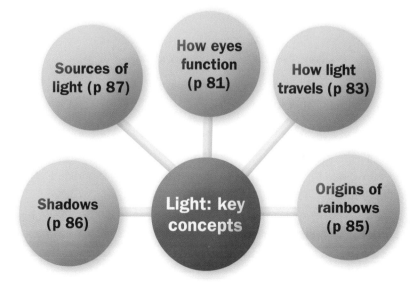

Key concept: how eyes function

Associated vocabulary

accommodation, blind spot, cones, cornea, dominant eye, iris, lens, monocular vision, optic nerve, pupil, retina, rods, stereoscopic vision, ultraviolet rays

Definitions

The eye is the organ of sight. The parts of the eye include the **cornea**, the **lens**, the **iris**, the **pupil**, the **retina** and the **optic nerve**. The human eye is a complex structure, as shown in Figure 8.1. It is covered by the cornea which, along with the lens, bends light rays as they enter the eye so that an image is recorded on the retina at the back of the eye. The retina is a light-sensitive tissue consisting of **rods** and **cones**. The rods produce a coarse, grey image under low levels of light, whereas the cones allow us to see fine detail and colour in daylight. The optic nerve sends the image captured on the retina to the brain to be processed. Human eyes have a **blind spot** where the optic nerve passes through the retina. Our brain compensates for this loss of image by using information from the other eye. Light enters the eye through the central opening called the pupil, which can vary in size depending on the amount of light available. The coloured part around the pupil is called the iris. Sunglasses and other protective eye wear should be worn to protect our eyes from the **ultraviolet rays** present in sunlight and while undertaking dangerous activities such as welding.

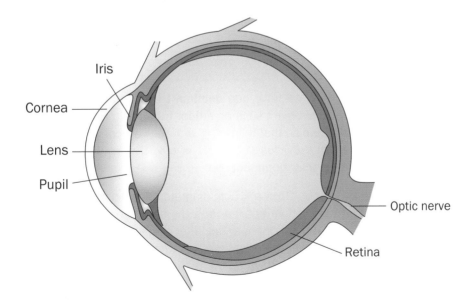

Figure 8.1 *Structure of the human eye.*

Examples

Our two eyes are centred on the front of our face so that different views can be captured. This **stereoscopic vision** provides a three-dimensional image of the world and allows us to judge distances. By making slight adjustments to the lens, our eyes can produce sharp images by a process known as **accommodation**.

Unlike humans, birds and lizards have **monocular** vision in which both eyes are used separately. Their eyes are positioned on the sides of their heads. This makes spotting predators easier as the field of view is greater, but the depth of their perception is reduced.

Some humans are colour blind. This is an inherited condition that limits an individual's ability to distinguish different colours. Many of us have to wear glasses – an additional lens which corrects our vision. People may be either short-sighted or long-sighted. When someone is short-sighted they can see nearby objects clearly, but cannot focus correctly on distant objects. Short-sightedness occurs when the distance between the lens and the retina is too large for an accurate image to be formed. When someone is long-sighted, they can see distant objects clearly, but cannot focus on nearby objects. Long-sightedness occurs when the distance between the lens and the retina is too short and the lens focuses the sharpest image behind the retina, rather than directly on it. This often occurs as people get older because the ageing process leads to a reduction in the elasticity of the lens.

Our eyes allow us to see images under a range of different lighting conditions because the iris can adjust the size of the pupil in response to either bright or dim light. This is a reflex action and, along with the blink reflex, is designed to protect our eyes. Tears are a slightly salty liquid secreted by the eyes to clean and lubricate them in response to irritation.

In practice

Year 6

To help children understand that we have one **dominant eye**, ask them to undertake the following activity. Select a vertical object such as a door frame and tell the children to hold their finger upright in front of them so that it lines up with the vertical object. Then ask them to observe what happens when they close each eye in turn. The eye for which their finger appears in the same position is their dominant eye.

You can also explore the blind spot. Draw a 1.5cm diameter black circle and a 2cm addition (plus) sign on a piece of A4 card, 16cm apart and at the same height in the middle of the page. Give each child the card and ask them to hold it at arm's length with the cross on the right. Then ask them to close or cover their right eye. Tell them to look only at the cross while slowly bringing the piece of card closer towards them. Get the children to discuss what they are seeing and why. Explain to the children that the spot seems to disappear when the light that is reflected from it falls on the blind spot in their left eye. Link this to what the children have learned about the anatomy of the eye and how the blind spot represents the point on the retina where the optic nerve is found.

Check your understanding

1. Can you name the main parts of the eye?

2. Can you explain how the eye records the images that are sent to the brain?

3. Can you think how children might be encouraged to make three-dimensional models of the eye?

4. Can you make a list of the health and safety issues to be covered when discussing sight?

Key concept: how light travels

Associated vocabulary

absorbed, concave, convex, electromagnetic radiation, energy, mirrors, opaque, photo-synthesis, reflect, refracted, transparent

Definitions

Visible light is a form of **electromagnetic radiation**. Light travels in straight lines from its source and can transmit **energy** from one place to another. Light, unlike sound, can travel through a vacuum. Light always travels at the same speed of 300,000 kilometres per second, which means that light from the Sun takes around eight minutes to reach the Earth.

Examples

When light hits an **opaque** surface, some of its energy is **absorbed** and can heat up the object. Light-coloured surfaces **reflect** light, which means that these objects stay cooler. These properties are used in hot countries, where solar cookers are made by painting tins black and houses are kept cool by painting them white. If light passes through a **transparent** material such as water or air, it may be bent or **refracted** and no longer follows a straight path. It is important that children realise that we see objects in daily life as a result of the rays of light coming towards our eyes from the light source. **Mirrors** reflect light from their silvered backing when the rays of light enter them. Light is reflected back at the same angle as it enters a mirror. This means that if the mirror is curved inwards (ie if it is **concave**), then objects will look smaller. If the mirror is **convex**, then objects will look taller. This is illustrated in Figure 8.2.

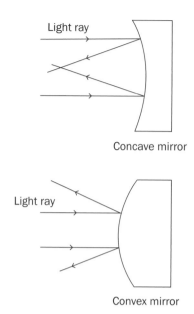

Figure 8.2 Light rays reflecting from concave and convex mirrors.

Solar panels are often used to capture energy from sunlight. Wafer-thin silicon cells convert this light energy into electrical energy. Plants absorb light through their green leaves and use this energy to make their own food via the process of **photosynthesis**.

In practice

Year 6

Children can explore how light moves away from its source in a straight line. Ask the children to take three pieces of strong A2 card and draw two diagonal lines from each of the opposing two corners of the card. Where the diagonal lines cross, make a small circular hole 1cm in diameter in the card. Using some clay to support the card, ask the children to place the cards 20cm apart on a table so that the holes are not lined up. Now darken the room and ask the children to use a strong flashlight to shine light through the first card. The children will see that the light from the flashlight cannot move along the card line because the second card now blocks the light. Now ask the children to arrange the cards so that light can be seen through all the holes. This should help the children to see that light travels in a straight line. You can then ask the children to follow up this activity by considering how they can bend rays of light using mirrors and prisms.

Check your understanding

1.   Can you explain what light is?

2.   Can you list the key terms linked to the study of light?

3.   Can you think of ways in which children might be encouraged to use other media to explore the properties of light?

Key concept: origins of rainbows

Associated vocabulary

electromagnetic radiation, prisms, reflected, refracted, spectrum, white light

Definitions

A rainbow is a multi-coloured arc in the sky formed when **white light** is both **reflected** and **refracted** from water droplets (such as mist and fog) in the atmosphere. The water droplets act like miniature **prisms,** splitting the white light into its constituent colours. Red is seen on the top outer edge of the rainbow, followed downwards by orange, yellow, green, blue, indigo and violet. This is the **spectrum** of white light.

Examples

If, on a sunny day, you stand by a large waterfall that creates a lot of spray, you will see a rainbow as the sunlight is split into a spectrum of different colours. Sir Isaac Newton is attributed with identifying the seven colours of the visible spectrum by using a prism to split white light. Visible light, however, forms just one small part of the whole spectrum of **electromagnetic radiation**. Different types of radiation are characterised by different wavelengths. Other forms of electromagnetic radiation include gamma rays, X-rays and ultraviolet radiation, which all have shorter wavelengths than visible light. Infrared radiation, microwaves and radio waves have longer wavelengths than visible light.

In practice

Year 6

Demonstrate that white light is made up of different colours with this simple experiment. Ask the children to cut out a circular disc 15cm in diameter from a thick piece of card. Using a pencil and protractor, ask them to divide both faces of the circular disc into seven equally sized and positioned segments. The children should then colour each segment of both faces with one of the following seven colours: red, orange, yellow, green, blue, indigo and violet. When they have done this, ask the children to make two small holes through the wheel near its centre, about 1cm apart, and then to push a piece of string 25cm long through each hole. Tell the children to tie up both ends of the string and then to wind the string up by swinging it as though they were using a skipping rope. If the children then pull the string tight, then the wheel will spin quickly in a circular motion. Encourage them to see that when the wheel spins, the colours blend and appear to be almost white.

Check your understanding

1. Can you explain how a rainbow is formed?
2. Can you name, in order, the seven colours that make up a rainbow?

3. Can you help the children to learn a mnemonic so they can remember the colours in a rainbow?

4. Can you come up with your own practical activity so children can make their own rainbows?

Key concept: shadows

Associated vocabulary

opaque, penumbra, translucent, transparent, umbra

Definitions

A shadow is formed when the passage of light is blocked by an object. A **transparent** object cannot produce a shadow because it allows light to pass through it; however, an **opaque** or **translucent** object will create a shadow. An opaque object creates a dark shadow and a translucent object creates a faint shadow. When the object is close to the light source, large shadows with a fuzzy edge are formed, whereas smaller, sharper images are formed when the object is close to the surface onto which the light is projected. The central and darkest part of a shadow is called the **umbra**, while the fuzzy grey edge is called the **penumbra**.

Examples

Shadows have been useful to humans throughout history. For example, people used shadows to tell the time long before watches were invented. Early civilisations such as the Egyptians created sundials, which can be used to tell the time by measuring the length and direction of shadows. Shadow puppets were used to entertain people long before moving images were used in cinema films.

The Sun is our major source of light and shadows are created when it shines. The Sun casts long shadows at the start and end of the day, but at midday, when the Sun is at its highest point in the sky, the shadows are much shorter.

In practice

Year 3

To investigate shadow formation, ask the children to create a shadow puppet show. Ask them to draw images of their characters on pieces of cardboard and then attach the cardboard images to pieces of dowelling. Put a bright lamp or light source on a table behind a translucent screen made from greaseproof paper. Darken the room and then ask the children to move their puppets between the light source and the back of the screen. Children will realise that if they move the puppet closer to the screen, then the image will become smaller and sharper, whereas larger blurred images are formed if the puppet is closer to the light source.

Check your understanding

1. Can you explain how a shadow is formed?

2. Can you explain how an image on a screen changes as it is moved closer and then further away from the light source?

3. Can you help the children design and make a sundial?

Key concept: sources of light

Associated vocabulary

primary source, produce, reflect, secondary source

Definitions

Primary sources of light, such as the Sun or a light bulb, are able to **produce** light from either electrical or chemical energy. **Secondary sources** of light, such as the Moon, do not produce light themselves, but **reflect** light from another source. Light, unlike sound, can travel through a vacuum.

Examples

Some sources of light, such as the Sun, light bulbs and fire, also produce heat. Other sources of light – for example, glow sticks and glow worms, which produce light by chemical reactions – almost produce no heat. Secondary sources of light include the Moon, the reflective strips worn by cyclists, and mirrors. Light sources are much easier to see if there is no other source of light nearby – for example, the stars are still present in the sky during the day, but we cannot see them because the light from our Sun is so much brighter than the stars.

In practice

Year 3

Take the children on a 'light hunt' around the school to look for sources of light. Can they find different sources of light inside and outside the school? Ask them to sort these lights into primary and secondary sources. Ask the children to think in terms of which sources of light are dangerous and which are safe to use. Make certain that they are aware of the dangers of looking directly at bright lights such as the Sun.

Create a dark-room in the classroom using either thick dark paper or thick material secured around a desk. Provide the children with a range of materials, such as a flashlight, glow stick, plastic mirror and a reflective strip. Ask the children to sort objects into primary and secondary sources of light in this small dark-room. The children could then be asked to carry out some research into how these objects produce and reflect light.

Check your understanding

1. Can you explain the difference between primary and secondary sources of light?

2. Can you name some primary and secondary sources of light?

3. Can you devise some activities to ensure children are safe when looking at bright sources of light?

9 Forces, motion and magnets

What do you need to know to be able to teach this topic?

Forces are not directly mentioned at Key Stage 1, but the topic could be covered when investigating the uses of everyday materials because the national curriculum (DfE 2013) states that pupils should be able to:

- *find out how the shapes of solid objects made from some materials can be changed by squashing, bending, twisting and stretching*

(DfE, 2013: 153)

Forces and motion are directly outlined in Key Stage 2 and pupils should be taught to:

- *compare how things move on different surfaces*

(DfE, 2013: 160)

- *explain that unsupported objects fall towards the Earth because of the force of gravity acting between the Earth and the falling object*

(DfE, 2013: 170)

- *identify the effects of air resistance, water resistance and friction, that act between moving surfaces*

- *recognise that some mechanisms, including levers, pulleys and gears, allow a smaller force to have a greater effect*

(DfE, 2013: 171)

To complement the study of forces, children should be given the opportunity to learn about magnets and the forces associated with them:

–   *notice that some forces need contact between two objects, but magnetic forces can act at a distance*

–   *describe magnets as having two poles*

–   *predict whether two magnets will attract or repel each other, depending on which poles are facing*

–   *compare and group together a variety of everyday materials on the basis of whether they are attracted to a magnet, and identify some magnetic materials*

–   *observe how magnets attract or repel each other and attract some materials and not others*

(DfE, 2013: 160)

SUBJECT KNOWLEDGE AUDIT

Use the following audit to identify the strengths and areas for development in your subject knowledge of this topic.

Using a scale of 1–4, rate your current level of competence:

1 = Excellent; 2 = Good; 3 = Satisfactory; 4 = Needs improvement.

	1	2	3	4
Define the term force				
Define the term gravity				
Define the term friction				
List and define the terminology linked to magnets				
Explain which materials are magnetic				
Describe where forces may be found in our daily lives				
Name a scientist linked to the science of forces				
Explain what a lever is				

Explain what a gear is				
Explain what a pulley is				
Define how you can quantify units of force				

FORCES, MOTION AND MAGNETS: CONCEPT MAP

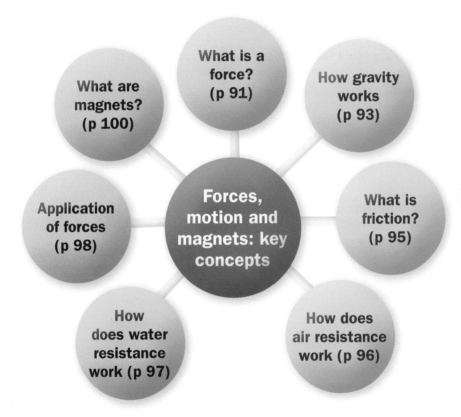

Key concept: what is a force?

Associated vocabulary

bend, direction, force, force meter, push, pull, magnitude, newton, opposing force, squash, stretch, twist

Definitions

A **force** interacts with an object and is able to change the movement of the object. It has a both a **magnitude** (size or strength) and a **direction**. Forces are usually described as a **push** or a **pull**. Forces can also **squash**, **bend**, **twist** and **stretch** an object.

Examples

From an early age, pupils will be familiar with how they can move an object such as a ball. However, they may not have thought about the vocabulary associated with this activity. They need to be aware that forces have a **magnitude** (size) and that this magnitude will affect how far an object will move. Forces also act in a particular direction, so if a ball is kicked from left to right, then it will move from left to right. Pupils should also be taught that forces are measured using a **force meter** and that the unit of force is a **newton**.

All forces have an **opposing force**, although this may not always be evident. For example, if an apple is lying on a table, then there is a downward force from gravity acting on the apple, but also an upward force from the table. The balance of these two opposing forces determines whether or not the object will move.

In practice

Year 2

The following activity helps young children to understand that forces vary in their magnitude and that non-standard units, such as finger lengths or hand spans, can be used to measure these forces. Provide the children with:

- a thick elastic band;
- a piece of dowel;
- a paperclip;
- a range of objects of different weights.

Open up the paperclip to make a hook and secure it to one end of the dowel. Ask a child to feel the force needed to move a selected object on a surface by using their hand to pull the item. Also ask the children to carefully stretch the elastic band so they can feel how their pull is resisted by the opposing force generated by the elastic band. Next, ask the children to place the elastic band around the object and to hook it onto the paperclip. Then ask them to record how much each object stretches the elastic band using non-standard measurements. The pupils will learn that the heavier the object, then the greater pull (force) that is needed to move it. Pupils could draw the experiment using different sized arrows on a diagram to illustrate the various forces. If you wish to develop this activity even further, you can then give pupils force meters to quantify the forces in newtons.

Check your understanding

1. Can you define a force?

2. Can you describe how we can quantify forces?

3. Can you explain how forces are paired?

Key concept: how gravity works

Associated vocabulary

force, gravity, gravitational pull, mass, Sir Isaac Newton, weight

Definitions

Gravity is an attractive force between objects that have **mass**. Most people recognise it as the force that pulls objects towards the centre of the Earth. The force of gravity is larger between objects of heavier mass, but becomes smaller as the distance between objects increases. A heavy object such as the Sun exerts a strong **gravitational pull**, whereas gravity on the Moon is only one-sixth of that on Earth because the Moon is so much smaller. This means that an object on the Moon will have a smaller **weight** than the same object on Earth (although it will have the same mass).

Examples

Sir Isaac Newton was an English physicist and mathematician who was born in 1643. He is probably best remembered for his work on gravity, which was published in 1687 in his book *Philosophiae Naturalis Principia Mathematica*. Children are often told that he discovered gravity when an apple fell on his head while he was sitting under a tree.

An object's weight is a measure of how much gravity is pulling down on the object. Weight is a **force** and is measured in newtons (abbreviated to N). The force of the Earth's gravity acting on 1kg of mass is roughly 10N. The mass of an object does not change, but its weight will be different under different gravitational forces. However, because we all live on Earth, we all experience the same gravitational force and so our weight is the same everywhere on our planet.

In practice

Year 5

Tell the pupils the story about Sir Isaac Newton discovering gravity when an apple fell on his head, or show them a short video clip relating to this story. Provide pupils with a copy of Figure 9.1.

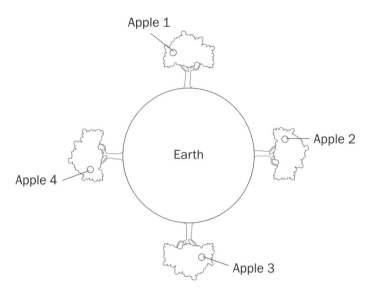

Figure 9.1 *Gravity can be represented by apples falling from trees. The apples will fall towards the centre of the Earth.*

Ask the children to imagine what would happen if the apple shown on each apple tree fell off and to draw pictures of what they think will happen. Some children will draw the apples falling in a straight line towards the centre of the Earth, while others will not be able to understand that objects fall towards the centre of the Earth and their apples will be drawn as in Figure 9.2.

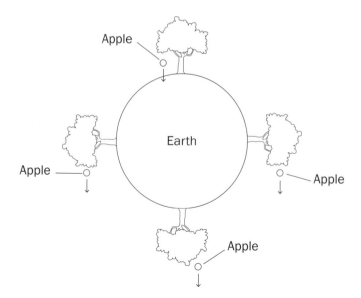

Figure 9.2 *Common misconception of gravity. Some children will draw the apples falling downwards, rather than towards the centre of the Earth.*

If the children draw the apples falling like this, ask them what would happen to an apple that fell off a tree in Australia. Would the apple really fall off the Earth into space? Follow this idea up using a globe of the Earth.

Check your understanding

1. Can you define gravity?

2. What is the force acting on 1kg of mass on the Earth's surface?

3. Can you explain how objects fall when they are in different places on the Earth's surface?

Key concept: what is friction?

Associated vocabulary

force, friction, frictional forces, resists

Definitions

Friction is a **force** that **resists** the movement of surfaces moving across each other. Friction always works in the opposite direction to the moving object and always acts to slow the object down.

Examples

The amount of friction depends on types of surface moving across each other. For example, if you try and push a toy car along on a wooden floor, it will go further and be easier to push than the same car on a carpet. When objects encounter **frictional forces**, heat is generated. For example, if children rub the palms of their hands quickly over each other, they will start to feel their hands warming as a result of friction. Some frictional forces can be beneficial to humans – for example, friction helps a tyre to grip the road and patterns on the soles of our shoes prevent us from slipping. Sometimes we want to reduce frictional forces – for example, using a plastic sledge to go faster downhill in the snow, or using oil to lubricate an engine so that it does not overheat.

In practice

Year 5

This activity will engage children to think about the role of friction in their daily lives. You will need:

- a small plastic bottle;

- some washing up liquid;

- some cooking oil;
- a pair of rubber gloves;
- a paper towel;
- some sandpaper.

Tell the children that they are going to repeatedly open the bottle using each of the items given to them. Ask them to predict which material will help them the most. Encourage them to think about the properties of each item. First, ask them to try to open the bottle after the lid has been smeared with cooking oil. The children will find it slips very easily and is almost impossible to open. Next, ask them to use the paper towel, then the rubber gloves and, lastly, the sandpaper. The children will soon realise that, as the surface of the material used to open the bottle becomes less smooth, the bottle will open more easily. This can then be discussed in terms of the properties of the items and the amount of friction they provide when opening the lid.

Make sure that the bottle lid is always screwed on very tightly after each experiment. After using the oil, clean the bottle lid with water to which the washing up liquid has been added and dry carefully.

Check your understanding

1. Can you define friction?
2. Can you list some advantages and disadvantages of friction in our daily lives?

Key concept: how does air resistance work?

Associated vocabulary

aerodynamics, air resistance, burn up, frictional force, heat energy, kinetic energy, streamlining

Definitions

Air resistance is a **frictional force** that acts against a moving object. As an object moves through the air, it pushes the particles of air out of its way. The opposing force from these particles makes it harder for the object to move through the air and slows it down. The amount of air resistance is determined by the speed of the object – the faster the object is moving, the greater the air resistance.

Examples

Air resistance works in opposition to the direction of movement – for example, it will slow down a lorry driving on a motorway. All moving objects have **kinetic energy** as a result of their movement and air resistance changes this energy into **heat energy**. For example, when a piece of space debris, such as a meteor, enters the Earth's atmosphere, the air resistance acting on the rapidly moving object causes it to heat up and we see it as a bright shooting star. We say that the object will **burn up** as it falls to Earth.

Sometimes air resistance can be of benefit to humans. For example, a parachute made of strong, light nylon will have a high air resistance, which means that the person attached to it falls slowly and safely back down to Earth. However, sometimes air resistance can have disadvantages. For example, a lorry will encounter greater air resistance at higher speeds, which will increase its fuel consumption. To help overcome this, lorries are often fitted with spoilers. This improves their **aerodynamics**, **streamlining** their shape and reducing air resistance.

In practice

Year 5

Children need to understand that air resistance is responsible for slowing objects down as they fall to Earth. A simple activity to demonstrate this involves a heavy A4-sized book and an A4 piece of paper that is just a little smaller than the cover of the book. Ask the children to predict which object will fall to the ground the fastest when dropped. Ask them to explain their thinking. Then, safely standing on a step, hold both items up and drop them at the same time. The children will no doubt be correct in saying that the light piece of paper will fall more slowly than the book. Next, repeat the activity, but this time place the piece of A4 paper on top of the book before you drop it. The children will be surprised to notice that they now fall at the same speed. Ask the children to explain what they think is happening in terms of air resistance.

Check your understanding

1. Can you explain what air resistance is?

2. Can you provide examples of air resistance in our everyday lives?

Key concept: how does water resistance work?

Associated vocabulary

bow, drag, eddies, force, frictional force, surface area, water resistance

Definitions

Water resistance is a **frictional force** that acts against a moving object. As an object moves through water, it pushes the molecules of water out of its way. The opposing force from these molecules makes it harder for the object to move through the water and slows it down.

Examples

Children can feel the effect of water resistance as they try and walk through water in a swimming pool. It is also the **force** responsible for slowing them down when they jump into the water. If we dive properly, shaped like a spear or torpedo, we will only make a small splash. This is because we have entered the water in a streamlined shape with a small **surface area**, which minimises the water resistance. However, if we do a 'belly flop' and our body has a large surface area when we hit the water, we create a larger splash. This is because our body is pushing a larger number of water particles out of the way, creating a larger amount of resistance. Streamlining allows boats, fish and whales to move more efficiently through water and reduces **drag**. These examples are all curved and narrow at their front end so they can cut through the water more easily.

In practice

Year 5

To allow pupils to investigate how a boat moves in a liquid, provide them with a large water tray filled with water, some modelling clay, some plastic straws and A4 paper. Suggest to the pupils that they are boat designers and need to investigate whether a boat with a flat front (**bow**) will move more easily through water than a boat with a pointed bow. Then ask small groups of pupils to use modelling clay to create a range of boat shapes and to create simple sails using plastic straws and paper. Ask them to predict which boat will move through the water most easily and why.

Help pupils to realise that, to have a fair test, they must keep the other conditions constant, such as the amount of modelling clay used. If you want pupils to see the effect of the drag created by each boat, you can sprinkle some homemade confetti on the water surface to show the way each boat forms **eddies** as it pushes the water out of its way.

Check your understanding

1. Can you explain what water resistance is?
2. Can you explain how boats are designed to overcome water resistance?
3. Can you use a swimming lesson to explain the concept of water resistance?

Key concept: application of forces

Associated vocabulary

fulcrum, gears, levers, pivot, pulleys

Definitions

Humans have found many ways to harness forces in everyday life. The three most common examples are the use of **levers**, **pulleys** and **gears**.

- Levers are stiff rods that sit on a **pivot** or **fulcrum** so that a heavy load secured on one end of the rod can be moved more easily by pressing down on the opposite end of the rod.

- A pulley is a machine in which a chain or rope is pulled over one or more wheels to help lift a load.

- A gear is a circular toothed wheel which interlocks with another similar wheel to change the speed and direction of movement.

Examples

An example of a lever is the use of a screwdriver to open a tin of paint. Pulleys are used to raise a bucket from a well or to lift an engine out of a car. Water wheels provide an excellent example of how gears can be used to change the direction of motion from the moving water to the grindstone, to increase or decrease the speed of a shaft, or to provide the power to lift sacks of flour.

In practice

Year 5

To help children understand how a lever can be useful in everyday life, ask them to use the end of a spoon to take the lid off a tin of syrup. You can also ask them to explain how a see-saw uses a pivot to move. Similarly, to help children understand the basic idea of a pulley, allow the pupils to throw a rope over a secure tree branch so they can feel how it can help them to lift a bucket of water off the ground.

Pupils will have encountered the idea of gears on bicycles, but may be less familiar with other uses of gears. Bring an old-fashioned whisk into the classroom so that the children can study how gears can be used to change the direction of movement. This knowledge can be developed in lessons such as design technology, when pupils could be encouraged to make a waterwheel and use gears to produce a rotary or circular motion.

Check your understanding

1. Can you explain what a pulley is and how it can be useful?

2. Can you explain what a gear is and how it can be useful?

3. Can you explain what a lever is and how it can be useful?

Key concept: what are magnets?

Associated vocabulary

cobalt, electromagnets, iron, lodestone, magnet, magnetic field, magnetite, nickel, permanent magnets, Northern Lights, north pole, south pole, steel, temporary magnets

---

Definitions

A **magnet** attracts magnetic materials such as **steel** and **iron**. Magnets are surrounded by a **magnetic field**.

Examples

Magnetic minerals such as **magnetite** (**lodestone**) are found naturally in rocks or can be made using magnetic materials such as iron, **nickel** and **cobalt**. The bar magnets used in schools are examples of **permanent magnets**. Permanent magnets remain magnetic all the time. **Temporary magnets** can be formed by passing an electric current through a conductor; however, once the electricity is turned off, the magnet will lose its strength. Temporary magnets are used to move iron in scrapyards. These types of magnets are called **electromagnets**. All magnets generate a **magnetic field**, as shown in Figure 9.3.

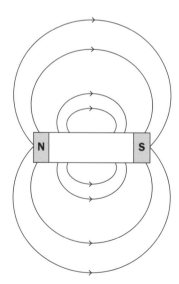

Figure 9.3 *Magnetic field around a bar magnet.*

This simple diagram shows that the magnetic field comes out of the end of the magnet, through the magnet's **north pole** and returns into the magnet via its **south pole**. The Earth's metallic core produces a magnetic field that allows us to navigate using a compass. The spectacular **Northern Lights** seen at high latitudes occur when charged particles from the Sun interact with the Earth's magnetic field.

In practice

Year 3

Magnets are attracted to iron and steel, but not all magnets have the same strength. To help pupils with this idea, provide them with a range of different sizes and shapes of magnets, some paperclips and a 30cm ruler. Ask the pupils to place the paperclips next to the 0cm mark on the ruler and then place the magnets at the 30cm end of the ruler. Tell the pupils to slowly move each magnet in turn towards the paperclip. When the paperclip is pulled towards the magnet, ask the children to record the distance at which it was attracted to the magnet. You could ask the pupils to do this several times to make it a fair test. When the children have all their readings, they can create a graph to show the strength of each magnet.

Check your understanding

1. Can you state which metals are magnetic?

2. Can you explain the difference between temporary and permanent magnetism?

3. Can you use a compass to work out which direction is north and south from your school?

10 Sound

What do you need to know to be able to teach this topic?

Sound is not directly mentioned at Key Stage 1 in the national curriculum (DfE 2013), but it could be covered when investigating the senses.

-   *identify, name, draw and label the basic parts of the human body and say which part of the body is associated with each sense*

    (DfE, 2013: 149)

However, in lower Key Stage 2, the national curriculum (DfE 2013) suggests that pupils should be taught to:

-   *identify how sounds are made, associating some of them with something vibrating*

-   *recognise that vibrations from sounds travel through a medium to the ear*

-   *find patterns between the volume of a sound and the strength of the vibrations that produced it*

-   *find patterns between the pitch of a sound and the features of the object that produced it*

-   *recognise that sounds get fainter as the distance from the sound source increases*

    (DfE, 2013: 163).

SUBJECT KNOWLEDGE AUDIT

Use the following audit to identify the strengths and areas for development in your subject knowledge of this topic.

Using a scale of 1–4, rate your current level of competence:

1 = Excellent; 2 = Good; 3 = Satisfactory; 4 = Needs improvement.

	1	2	3	4
Describe how sound is made				
Describe how sound travels				
Explain what volume is				
Explain what pitch is				
Name the parts of the human ear				
Describe the dangers associated with sound				
Explain what an echo is				

SOUND: CONCEPT MAP

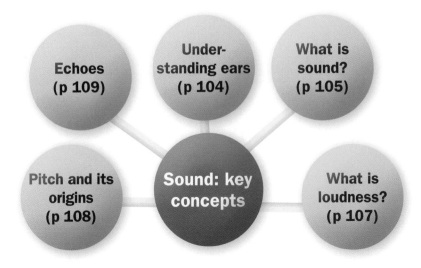

Key concept: understanding ears

Associated vocabulary

anvil, auditory nerve, balance, binaural hearing, cochlea, ear, ear canal, ear drum, hammer, hearing, inner ear, middle ear, outer ear, oval window, pinna, semi-circular canals, stirrup

Definitions

The **ear** is the organ that provides the sense of **hearing** and also helps humans and other vertebrates with their **balance**.

Examples

The ear consists of three parts: the **outer ear**, the **middle ear** and the **inner ear** (Figure 10.1). The outer ear or **pinna** helps to collect sounds and channels them along the **ear canal**. The sounds then strike the **ear drum** and cause it to vibrate. These vibrations are made more intense in the middle ear as they are transferred in turn from the **hammer** to the **anvil** and then to the **stirrup.** The stirrup is attached to the **oval window**, which contains a membrane attached to the **cochlea**. As the sound vibrations enter the cochlea in the inner ear, they cause tiny hairs to move as the sound vibrations travel along this fluid-filled organ. This leads to the creation of electrochemical signals, which are transferred by the **auditory nerve** to the brain to be interpreted as sound. The inner ear also contains **semi-circular canals**, which are filled with fluid and help to control balance.

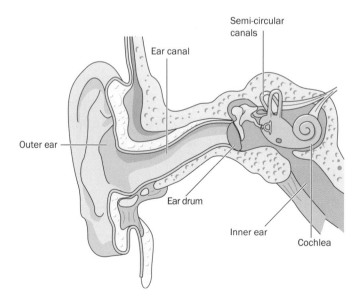

Figure 10.1 *Structure of the human ear.*

Examples

Humans, unlike many animals, cannot locate sounds by moving their outer ears. However, they can accurately locate sounds using both ears and this is known as **binaural hearing**. Animals can hear a much wider range of sounds than humans – for example, cats can hear very high-pitched sounds, which helps them to locate their prey. It is important that we are careful with our hearing. If we are exposed to sustained high levels of noise in either short bursts or over long periods of time, then this can lead to temporary or permanent hearing loss. Children should be reminded to look after their hearing and not to poke anything into their ears or to shout loudly into another person's ear

In practice

Year 4

To help children understand that the outer ear has a very important role to play in our hearing, ask them to listen for different sounds in and around the school. Ask them to consider if they are faint, loud, high- or low-pitched sounds. Next, provide the children with an A2 piece of card and ask them to roll this into a cone with at least a 30cm outer diameter and a 2cm diameter at the tapered end. Secure the cone with sticky tape. Tell the children to safely place the narrow end to their ear. If necessary, adjust it so that it is a snug fit before they start to listen to different sounds in and around the school. Ask them to describe what they hear. They should notice that the sounds are now much easier to hear. Explain to the children that this is because the cone is now making their hearing more directional as its large conical shape collects the sounds more easily than their small, flattened ears. You could then ask children to research which animals have large conical-shaped ears and why this adaptation might be useful.

Check your understanding

1. Can you name some of the parts of the ear?
2. Can you explain how the ear sends messages to the brain?
3. Can you find any videos that might support the teaching of hearing?
4. Can you make a list of the health and safety issues to be covered when discussing hearing?

Key concept: what is sound?

Associated vocabulary

compression, longitudinal waves, medium, molecule, particles, rarefraction, sound, vibrations

Definitions

Sound consists of **longitudinal waves** or **vibrations** transferred by a **medium** such as air or water. When the wave or vibration is created, it moves away from the original disturbance that created the vibration.

Examples

Sound, like light, can transmit energy. Humans can hear sounds transmitted through air, although the vibrations that cause these sounds cannot be seen. Sound waves are longitudinal waves that travel away from their source, but they need a medium to travel through – sound cannot travel through a vacuum. When a drum is hit, the skin moves and pushes the air **particles** above it closer together. This is known as **compression**. As the drum skin moves back to its rest position, the particles near it are now more spread out than the particles that had been compressed. This is known as **rarefraction**. This sound wave moves outwards from the drum as particles are repeatedly compressed and then returned to their normal state, as shown in Figure 10.2.

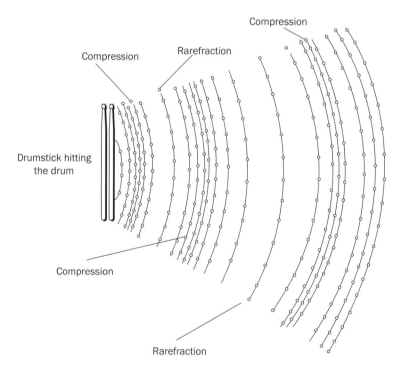

Figure 10.2 *Representational diagram showing the compression and rarefraction of air particles as a sound wave is transmitted.*

Children will associate sounds with many objects, but the example of a guitar string will help them make a direct link between the vibration caused by plucking it and the sound from the guitar. Sometimes the vibrations caused by very low sounds can actually be felt – for example, when a low bass note is played through loudspeakers or when a fog horn is blown.

Sounds are transmitted through different solids, liquids and gases at different speeds. In a solid, sounds travel at about 6000 metres per second, at 1500 metres per second in a liquid and at 330 metres per second in a gas.

In practice

Year 4: sound waves

As we cannot see sound waves moving through the air, this activity allows children to model this concept in a practical way. Ask two children to take the ends of a slinky spring and to move apart so that the spring is stretched out between them, but not tightly. Tell the children to both kneel down and to hold their end on the ground. One child should then give their end a sharp push or flick to represent the disturbance that creates a sound. Encourage the children to describe what they see. By making close observations, they should notice that the spring is compressed and then extended during the movement of the wave along the spring. You can liken this compression and extension to that of the air particles being compressed and then released as the sound wave travels outwards from its source.

Check your understanding

1.   Can you explain what sound is?
2.   Can you list the key terms linked with the study of sound?
3.   Can you think how children might be encouraged to name a variety of sources of sound in their surroundings?

Key concept: what is loudness?

Associated vocabulary

amplitude, decibels, loudness

Definitions

The **loudness** of a sound is proportional to the **amplitude** of the sound wave, as shown in Figure 10.3. If the amplitude (the amount of movement of the medium) is large, then a loud sound is heard. Small amplitudes result in quieter sounds.

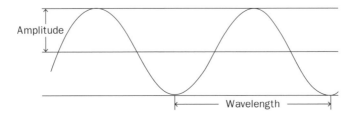

Figure 10.3 *Amplitude and wavelength of a longitudinal wave.*

Examples

Children have some awareness of loudness from an early age. They may have played an instrument and understand that when something is hit, blown or struck, if more force is applied to the instrument, then a louder sound will be produced. This gives them an insight into the idea that different amounts of energy are involved in producing loud and soft sounds. The standard units used to measure the loudness of sound are **decibels** (dB).

In practice

Year 4

Give a pair of pupils a drumstick, a drum and a handful of rice. Take the children outside and ask one pupil to stand at one end of the outside space while the other pupil takes the drum, drumstick and rice to the other end. Make certain that the pupil with the drum is far enough away so the drum cannot be heard if it is struck lightly. Ask the child to keep increasing the force with which the drum is hit until the other child puts up their hand to indicate that they have heard the drum. Then ask them to swap roles. Pupils undertaking this activity will quickly realise that the more intense a beat or input of energy, then the louder the sound. To show pupils that striking the drum harder makes the drum skin move more, place the rice on the drum skin. They will notice that the rice jumps higher when they hit the drum with more force.

Check your understanding

1. Can you explain the meaning of amplitude?
2. Can you explain the relationship between the vibrations that create a sound and the loudness of the sound produced?
3. Can you find other ways of showing the link between the amount of vibration and loudness?

Key concept: pitch and its origins

Associated vocabulary

frequency, Hertz, infrasound, pitch, sonar, ultrasound, unpitched, sonar, wavelength

Definitions

The **pitch** of a sound is how high or low it is. The pitch of a sound is determined by its **frequency**, which is a measure of how many sound waves pass a particular point in space in a unit of time. Frequency is measured in units of **Hertz** (Hz). The **wavelength** of a wave (Figure 10.3) is the distance between a point on one wave and an identical point on the next wave.

Examples

Both animals and humans are capable of detecting a wide range of frequencies or different pitches. The human ear is capable of hearing sounds in the range 20–20,000Hz. Sound below a frequency of 20Hz is called **infrasound** and frequencies above 20,000Hz are called **ultrasound**. Some animals can hear much lower frequency sounds than us – for example, elephants can hear down to about 5Hz. Other animals can hear sounds in a much higher frequency range – for example, a bat can hear up to 120,000Hz. Bats produce ultrasonic waves that help them to navigate.

Musical instruments rely on a range of pitches to create the sounds we call music. Orchestras are composed of many **pitched** and some **unpitched** instruments. Cymbals are an example of an unpitched instrument and produce sounds of indeterminate pitch. Other percussion instruments such as timpani or kettle drums are pitched by adjusting the tightness of the drum skin. High-pitched notes have higher frequencies than low-pitched notes.

In practice

Year 4

The following activity will help children to understand how pitch can be changed. Ask the children to place a plastic 30cm ruler on their desk so that the most of it sticks out horizontally at a right angle to the edge of the desk. Ask the children to 'twang' the ruler (without breaking it) and listen to the pitch of sound created. Ask them to observe the behaviour of the ruler. Then ask them to repeat this after moving the ruler inwards towards the desk as it vibrates. Ask the children to describe how the vibrations and the pitch change. Pupils will notice that the pitch of the note produced becomes higher as the number of vibrations per second increases.

Check your understanding

1. Can you explain what pitch is?
2. Can you explain the difference between pitched and unpitched instruments?
3. Can you name a range of differently pitched instruments in an orchestra?

Key concept: echoes

Associated vocabulary

echo, echo location, reflected, sonar

Definitions

An **echo** is a repeated sound that is heard after the initial sound wave has been **reflected** from the surface of an object.

Examples

Although some children will have heard an echo, they may not have thought about what caused it. Echoes are most commonly heard when someone shouts against a wall, rock face or in an empty room. Echoes occur when the sound waves bounce back off a hard surface and are heard again by the listener. An echo can only be heard if the listener is at least 20m away from the hard surface. This is because humans can only hear two distinct sounds if they are at least 0.1s apart.

Echoes can occur in water as well as in air. As sound travels faster in water than in air, echoes are heard much quicker in water than in air. **Echo location** or **sonar** uses this idea to judge the depth of the sea bed. A transmitter on a ship emits a short pulse of sound, which travels outwards from the ship towards the seafloor. The sound is reflected back from the seafloor and recorded on board the ship. A computer is used to calculate the depth of water below the ship from the time taken for the pulse to be received back.

In practice

Although the concept of an echo is not part of the curriculum for Key Stage 2, an understanding of this concept will help your pupils with many of the ideas around sound. A good activity to help promote their understanding is to ask them to create their own echoes. Find a large room that has solid, flat surfaces and little, if any, soft furnishings as these may prevent the creation of an echo.

Ask the children to stand opposite each other in the space and ask them to clap loudly. They should hear their claps being reflected back to them. You can help children understand what is happening by telling them to think about a wave bouncing against a sea wall. Encourage the children to think about the delay in hearing the returned sound. Ask them to consider the link between this delay and the speed of sound. Would this delay be less if sound travelled faster? After this activity you could ask the pupils to try clapping in different areas around the school such as corners, facing the playground and near curtains or blinds. Does this change the likelihood of hearing an echo?

Check your understanding

1.   Can you explain what an echo is?

2.   Can you explain some useful applications of echoes – for example, sonar?

11   Electricity

What do you need to know to be able to teach this topic?

The national curriculum (DfE, 2013) places a statutory requirement on schools to teach pupils about electricity. It suggests pupils should be taught to:

- *identify common appliances that run on electricity*

- *construct a simple series electrical circuit, identifying and naming its basic parts, including cells, wires, bulbs, switches and buzzers*

- *identify whether or not a lamp will light in a simple series circuit, based on whether or not the lamp is part of a complete loop with a battery*

- *recognise that a switch opens and closes a circuit and associate this with whether or not a lamp lights in a simple series circuit*

- *recognise some common conductors and insulators, and associate metals with being good conductors*

                                                                        (DfE, 2013: 158)

- *associate the brightness of a lamp or the volume of a buzzer with the number and voltage of cells used in the circuit*

- *compare and give reasons for variations in how components function, including the brightness of bulbs, the loudness of buzzers and the on/off position of switches*

- *use recognised symbols when representing a simple circuit in a diagram*

                                                                        (DfE, 2013: 170)

SUBJECT KNOWLEDGE AUDIT

Use the following audit to identify the strengths and areas for development in your subject knowledge of this topic.

Using a scale of 1–4, rate your current level of competence:

1 = Excellent; 2 = Good; 3 = Satisfactory; 4 = Needs improvement.

	1	2	3	4
Know what electricity is and what uses electricity				
Be able to construct a simple series electrical circuit				
Know how a series electrical circuit works				
Identify and name basic parts of a circuit, eg cell, bulb, wire, switch and buzzer				
Understand the role of a switch in a simple series circuit				
Recognise and name common conductors and insulators				
Understand how the voltage of cells determines the brightness of a bulb or the volume of a buzzer				
Be able to give reasons for variations in how components function, eg the brightness of bulbs				
Know about conventional symbols used in circuit diagrams				
Understand what static electricity is				

ELECTRICITY: CONCEPT MAP

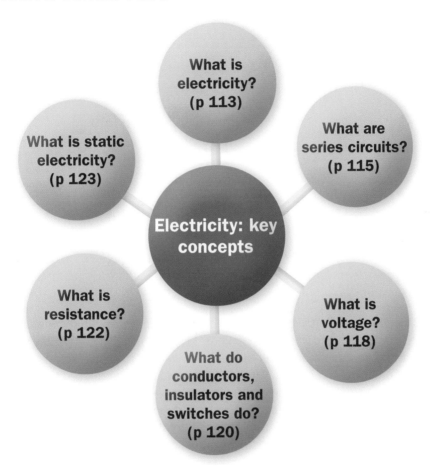

Key concept: what is electricity?

Associated vocabulary

atoms, battery, conductor, electric charge, electric current, electric shock, electrical circuit, electricity, electrons, energy, heat energy, kinetic energy, light energy, neutrons, nucleus, protons, sound energy, voltage

Definitions

Electricity is a form of **energy**. All matter is made up of small particles called **atoms**. Atoms are made up of three types of particle called **protons**, **neutrons** and **electrons** (Figure 11.1). The centre of an atom is called the **nucleus** and is made up of neutrons and protons. Neutrons have no charge and protons have a positive charge. Electrons orbit the nucleus and have a negative charge. An **electric current** is a moving flow of **electric charge**. In an **electrical**

circuit, the current is caused by a flow of electrons in a **conductor** such as a metal wire. An electric current requires both a source of chemical energy and a loop of conducting material that allows the transfer of energy.

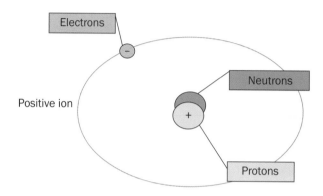

Figure 11.1 *Simple model of an atom.*

Examples

Electricity is used for heating, lighting and cooking and to power many other useful appliances such as computers and washing machines. Most of the electricity we use in our homes is mains electricity generated by power stations using fossil fuels, nuclear fission or renewable sources of energy such as wind, water or solar power. These are used to produce steam, which, in turn, is used to drive turbines connected to generators that produce an electric **voltage**. This electrical energy is distributed to homes and factories through high-voltage cables. The current generated by the mains supply is an alternating current – that is, it changes direction many times in a second. The electricity enters our homes at 240 volts. Electricity can be easily converted into other forms of energy such as **heat**, **light**, **sound** or **kinetic energy**.

Other electrical appliances such as torches use a **battery** as the source of energy. The batteries used in primary schools are safe because they only produce small amounts of electricity. Batteries produce a direct current – that is, a one-way flow of electrons – rather than an alternating current.

Precautions need to be taken when dealing with electricity as it can be dangerous and even deadly if misused. For example, touching a light switch with wet hands or playing near power lines can result in an **electric shock**. An electric shock occurs when a current passes through our body from an outside source. This affects the normal nervous impulses of our body. Muscle control may be lost and, if the current is large enough, it can cause our heart to stop beating.

In practice

Year 4

Ask the children to name different domestic appliances that use electricity. Ask them to research how electricity is generated by power stations using different sources of energy such as coal, oil, water or solar power and how it is then transmitted to our homes. They could discuss which sources of power are environmentally friendly. A comparison could be made about the relative safety of the electricity produced by a power station and that produced by a battery. They could research Michael Faraday, who invented the first dynamo to generate electricity in the 1830s.

Children could also bring in different items that use batteries (eg toys, calculators and torches) and describe how the electrical components (eg the alarm, motor or light) obtain power from the battery. Rechargeable batteries should be avoided in primary schools as they can cause short circuits.

A useful activity is to encourage pupils to reflect on the dangers of electricity – for example, by asking them to design a poster for a young audience.

Check your understanding

1. Can you define what electricity is?
2. Can you list some appliances that use electricity?
3. Can you explain the difference between mains electricity and electricity produced by a battery?
4. Do you know what an electric current is?
5. Can you explain some of the dangers of using electricity?

Key concept: what are series circuits?

Associated vocabulary

ampere, battery, bulb, buzzer, circuit, coulombs, conductor, energy, lamp, load, motor, series circuit

Definitions

A **series circuit** is an electrical **circuit** in which all the components, such as the **battery** and **bulb**, are connected end to end and form a single unbroken conducting path for electrons to flow around. An electric current has the following parts:

*   a power supply, such as a battery or a generator;
*   the **conductor** that carries the current;
*   the **load** or electrical device – for example, a **lamp**.

A lamp is the name given to the whole lighting device; the bulb is only the glass part. Figure 11.2 shows a simple series circuit in which the electricity travels in a circle from the battery, through the wire and back to the battery.

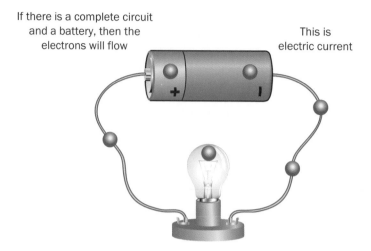

If there is a complete circuit and a battery, then the electrons will flow

This is electric current

Figure 11.2 *Simple series circuit.*

The electric current in a circuit is measured by the amount of charge that passes a particular point in a circuit in a given time in units of **coulombs**. When one coulomb of charge flows in one second the current is one **ampere** (1 amp or 1A). The electrons are not used up when the bulb is lit – it is the moving electrons or current that transfer **energy** from the battery to the bulb. It is this energy that is transferred to the bulb, not the electrons or the current. For a simple circuit with no branches the electrical current is the same at any point in the circuit.

The standard symbols for various components used in simple circuits are shown in Figure 11.3.

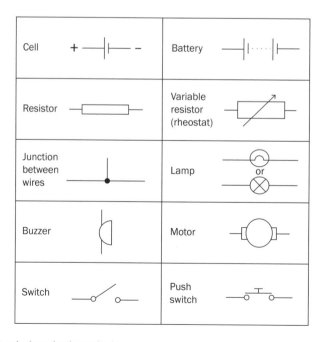

Figure 11.3 *Standard electrical symbols.*

Examples

Electricity passes through the thin wire, called a filament, in a light bulb. The filament is usually made of tungsten. The electrons transfer energy to the wire, which causes the filament to become very hot and glow. This is seen as visible light.

Other electrical devices such as **buzzers** or **motors** can also be used in a series circuit. The battery and buzzer, or the battery and motor, are connected in sequence and form one path for electrons to flow in an unbroken conducting path from, and back to, the power supply.

The buzzers used in schools often have a black wire and a red wire, which means that they have negative and positive terminals and need to be connected to a battery in a particular direction. The red wire in the buzzer is attached to the positive terminal of the battery and the black wire is attached to the negative terminal of the battery.

Inside a motor there is a coil of wire mounted between two magnets. When the current in the coil is turned on, the coil behaves like a magnet and moves. The current in the coil is reversed every half-turn. This is known as an alternating current and keeps the motor rotating in the same direction. If the wires at the terminals of the battery are swapped, this will reverse the direction of the magnetic field and the motor will move in the opposite direction.

In practice

Year 4

Ask the children to make different series circuits using a battery, two wires and a bulb and then substitute the bulb for a buzzer and then a motor. They should note what happens if the components are not connected end to end. Explain the functions of the different parts of the bulb so that they can also understand how electricity flows inside the bulb as well as round the circuit.

Next ask the pupils to attach the wires of the buzzer to the terminals of the battery and see what happens when the black wire is attached to the positive terminal and the red wire is attached to the negative terminal, and vice versa.

Make another circuit and attach a propeller to the motor, perhaps as part of something that has been built in design and technology, and prompt the pupils to change the wires at the terminals of the cell and notice how the direction of the propeller changes.

Children can record their series circuits by drawing them and labelling the component parts, or by taking photographs. In Year 6, they can use the recognised symbols shown in Figure 11.3.

Check your understanding

1. Can you explain why some circuits are called series circuits?

2. Do you know what an electric current is?

3.   Can you list the different parts of a series current and describe their functions?

4.   Can you explain how a bulb, buzzer and motor work in a series circuit?

Key concept: what is voltage?

Associated vocabulary

battery, cell, electric current, electrical potential energy, potential difference, negative terminal, positive terminal, volt, voltage, voltmeter

Definitions

A **voltage** is the difference in electrical potential between the **positive terminal** and the **negative terminal** in a battery. In an electrical circuit, the **battery** provides the electrons with **electrical potential energy**. A battery consists of a mixture of chemicals that react together and produce a surplus of electrons at the negative terminal of the battery and a shortage of electrons at the positive terminal of the battery. The correct term for a single battery is a **cell** and two or more cells connected together are called a battery (Figure 11.4).

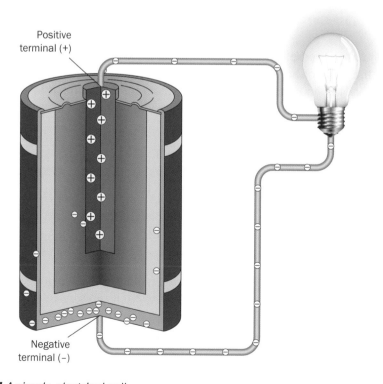

Positive
terminal (+)

Negative
terminal (−)

Figure 11.4 *A simple electrical cell.*

When a good electrical conductor such as a metal wire links the negative terminal of a battery to the positive terminal, the electrons in the wire start to move away from the negative terminal and are attracted towards the positive terminal. The movement of electrons through the wire causes an **electric current** to flow. If the electrons reach a bulb, some of their electrical potential energy is converted into heat and light in the bulb. The difference in electrical potential energy between the negative and positive terminals of a battery is the **potential difference**, or the voltage of the battery and is measured in **volts** using a **voltmeter**.

Examples

A water pump analogy is sometimes used to describe the role of a battery and how electricity flows around a circuit. Electricity is represented by water in a circular pipe and the battery is represented by a pump. A pump is needed to make the water flow around the pipe in the same way that a battery is needed to make electricity flow around a circuit. The water is always in the pipe, but a pump is needed to make the water move. As no water can leave the pipe, the amount of water leaving the pump every second must be the same as the amount of water returning to the pump. The bigger the pump (or the voltage of the battery), the more power it has and the faster the water (or the electricity) will move around the circuit. The battery does not create electricity, but provides energy to make the electric current move around the circuit.

The most commonly used batteries used in schools are 4.5V and are readily available. They are safe to use because they provide a low voltage and direct current and are convenient and easily portable. Batteries should never be cut open because they contain corrosive chemicals.

In practice

Year 6

Ask the children to make a circuit using a battery, two wires and a bulb. Then change the voltage of the battery and note what happens to the brightness of the bulb. Ask the children to describe what happened and to explain these changes. As the number of cells in a circuit increases, the voltage increases and the current becomes larger.

Next ask the children to make a circuit using three batteries and seven bulbs in series. All the bulbs will be lit, but ask the pupils to explain what would happen if one of the bulbs was faulty.

Show them a circuit made up of four batteries and one single bulb and ask them to predict what will happen. The bulb will light up for a short while, but the filament will quickly burn out and the bulb will blow because the voltage is too large.

The children could carry out some research about the creation of early batteries in 1800 by the Italian physicist Allessandro Volta and write an account in the form of a newspaper report.

Check your understanding

1. Can you explain the role of a battery in a simple circuit?

2. Are you confident in using the water pump analogy to describe the movement of electric current in a circuit?

3. Do you know what voltage is?

4. Do you understand what electrical potential energy is and why there is a difference between the positive and negative terminals of a battery?

5. Are you aware of some health and safety considerations when using batteries?

Key concept: what do conductors, insulators and switches do?

Associated vocabulary

copper, electrons, electrical conductors, electrical insulator, rubber, switch

Definitions

An **electrical conductor** is a material that allows electricity to flow through it. An **electrical insulator** is a material that does not allow electricity to flow through it. All metals, such as **copper**, are electrical conductors. On the atomic scale, metals form structures in which negatively charged **electrons** are free to move through the material. The flow of these free electrons can result in an electric current if a voltage is applied across the material. In an insulator, such as **rubber**, the electrons are not free to move and therefore a current does not flow.

A **switch** is a device that can complete or break a circuit. When the switch is closed (on), a current will flow because there is a continuous loop of conducting material connected to the battery. When the switch is open (or off), it breaks the circuit and the flow of current is stopped.

Examples

All metals allow electricity to flow through them and are therefore electrical conductors. Most non-metallic solids, such as plastic or wood, do not allow an electric current to pass through them and are known as electrical insulators. Some non-metal substances such as graphite, which is formed from layers of carbon atoms, also allow a current to pass through them.

Some liquids, such as water, also conduct electricity, but the currents produced are very small. The dangers of mixing electricity and water need to be emphasised – for example, touching an electrical switch with wet hands can result in an electric shock and even death.

In practice

Year 4

Set the children a task that involves testing a range of materials to determine whether electricity will flow through them and light a bulb or sound a buzzer. Ask them to insert the material in their circuit in the gap as shown in Figure 11.5 and attach the material with the two ends of the wire.

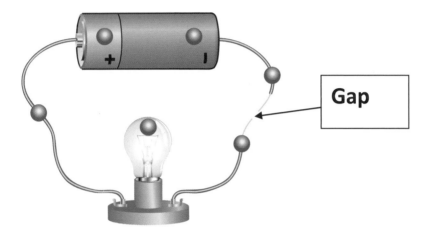

Figure 11.5 *Simple circuit to test whether a material is a conductor.*

Ask the pupils to predict which materials they think will be conductors and therefore light the bulb. They should record their predictions. Then carry out the tests to see whether their predictions were correct.

Insert a switch into the gap and ask the pupils to explain what happens to the current when the switch is opened and closed. Ask the children to experiment by making their own switches with two drawing pins and a paper clip (Figure 11.6). The components of the switch need to be electrical conductors to allow the current to flow through them.

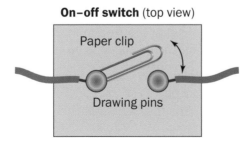

Figure 11.6 *A simple 'on–off' switch.*

Check your understanding

1. Can you provide a concise definition of what an electrical conductor is?

2. Can you provide a concise definition of what an electrical insulator is?

3. Can you provide examples of both conductors and insulators?

4. Can you explain how a switch works?

Key concept: what is resistance?

Associated vocabulary

conductors, current, electrons, load, ohms, resistance, series circuit, voltage

---

Definitions

Resistance measures how a device or material reduces the electric current flowing through it. Resistance tells us how much **voltage** is required to send a particular current through a component such as a bulb, alarm or buzzer. It is a measure of how difficult it is for a **current** to pass through a **load** in the circuit.

Resistance is measured in **ohms** (Ω). A resistance of 1Ω needs a voltage of 1V to push a current of 1A through it. All components have resistance and some have more resistance than others. The current that flows through each component depends on its resistance. The lower the resistance, the larger the current that will flow through the component for a given voltage. If the resistance is increased, less current will flow, or, alternatively, more voltage will be needed to keep the same current flowing. The relationship between current, voltage and resistance is known as Ohm's law.

Examples

Electrical **conductors** become warmer when an electric current is passed through them. The thickness of a conductor affects the ease with which the **electrons** move through it. A thinner wire has a greater resistance than a thicker wire made from the same material. Metals contain a large number of electrons that are free to move, so a relatively low voltage will produce a current. A variable resistor can be added to an electrical circuit to vary the amount of current flowing through it.

In practice

Year 6

Ask the children to modify the water pipe analogy to explain resistance in a circuit. Ask the pupils to describe what would happen if the pipe was narrower. There would be more resistance to the flow of the water (current). To maintain the same flow of water, you would need to install a bigger pump (increase the voltage).

The total resistance in a **series circuit** can be calculated by adding together all the resistances of all the components. Ask the children to connect a 3V battery and a bulb with a resistance of 4.5Ω in series and note the brightness of the bulb. Then ask them to add another 4.5Ω bulb to the series circuit and note what happens to the brightness of the bulbs. They should see that the two bulbs will glow less brightly than the single bulb as a result of the reduction in the current. Then ask the children to use a 6V battery with the two 4.5Ω bulbs. They will see that the two bulbs will now glow as brightly as the single 4.5Ω bulb in the first circuit.

Check your understanding

1.   Can you define resistance?

2.   Can you explain Ohm's law and the relationship between voltage, current and resistance?

3.   Can you work out the total resistance in a circuit?

Key concept: what is static electricity?

Associated vocabulary

atoms, attract, discharge, electrons, negatively charged, lightning, positively charged, repel, static electricity, voltages

---

Definitions

Static electricity is a stationary electric charge that is built up on an insulating material as a result of friction. It is produced when **electrons** are removed from the surface **atoms**, which makes the surface **positively charged**, or when electrons collect on the surface of materials, which makes the surface **negatively charged**.

Examples

In an electrical storm, different parts of the storm clouds can become charged with static electricity. This build-up of charge can be rapidly discharged as **lightning** either between or within clouds, or between the cloud and the Earth's surface. This **discharge** of static electricity as lightning can produce enormous **voltages**.

In practice

Ask the children to rub a plastic comb with a duster. Electrons from the atoms on the surface of the duster will spread out on the comb's surface, resulting in an excess of electrons on the comb – that is, a negative electric charge. If the comb is then brought close to pieces of paper, the extra electrons on the comb cause the electrons on the surface of the paper to move away because the negatively charged electrons **repel** each other. This means that the surface of the paper close to the comb will have a positive charge. The paper will be attracted to the comb because negative and positive charges **attract** each other.

Children can carry out research into the causes of thunder and lightning. Hypothetical examples could be provided so they could work out the distance of a storm by counting the number of seconds between seeing the lightning and hearing the thunder. Taking the number of seconds and dividing by 0.34 will tell them how far away the storm is in kilometres.

Check your understanding

1. Can you provide a concise definition of what static electricity is?

2. Can you give an example of how static electricity is produced?

3. Can you explain why lightning occurs?

Taking it further

Books and reports

Allen, M (2014) *Misconceptions in Primary Science*. 2nd edn. Maidenhead: Open University Press/ McGraw-Hill Education.

Association for Science Education (2010) *Be Safe!* 4th edn. Hatfield: Association for Science Education.

Chandler, F, Hancock, D and Woodcock, J (2004) *First Encyclopedia of the Human Body*. St Louis, MO: Turtleback Books.

Cooke, A and Howard, C (2014) *Practical Ideas for Teaching Primary Science*. Northwich: Critical Publishing.

Cross, A and Bowden, A (2009) *Essential Primary Science*. Maidenhead: Open University Press/ McGraw-Hill Education.

Daynes, K and King, K (2006) *See Inside Your Body*. London: Usborne.

Dove, J (1997) Geology and art: cross-curricular links. *Journal of Art and Design Education*, 16(2), 171–76.

Nuffield Primary Science: Key Stage 2 (1993) London: HarperCollins.

Parker, S (2009)*The Concise Human Body Book: an Illustrated Guide to its Structure, Function and Disorders*. London: Dorling Kindersley.

Peacock, G, Sharp, J, Johnsey, R and Wright, D (2014) *Primary Science Knowledge and Understanding*. 7th edn. London: Sage.

Wenham, M and Ovens, P (2010) *Understanding Primary Science*. 3rd edn. London: Sage.

Winston, R (2005) *Body: an Amazing Tour of Human Anatomy*. London: Dorling Kindersley.

Websites

Chapter 2: Animals and humans

www.bbc.co.uk/bitesize/ks2/science/living_things/ (accessed 5 February 2014).

www.bbc.co.uk/bitesize/ks2/science/living_things/moving_growing/play/ (accessed 5 February 2014).

www.bbc.co.uk/bitesize/ks2/science/living_things/teeth_eating/read/1/ (accessed 5 February 2014).

www.bbc.co.uk/bitesize/ks2/science/living_things/teeth_Eating/read/1/ (accessed 5 February 2014).

www.bbc.co.uk/education/topics/zcyycdm/videos/1 (accessed 5 February 2014).

www.bbc.co.uk/science/humanbody (accessed 5 February 2014).

www.nhs.uk/Livewell/dentalhealth/Pages/Careofkidsteeth.aspx (accessed 5 February 2014).

Chapter 3: Plants, habitats and living things

www.edenproject.com/learn (accessed 26 May 2015).

www.growingschools.org.uk/ (accessed 27 May 2015).

http://resources.woodlands-junior.kent.sch.uk/revision/science/living/ (accessed 26 May 2015).

www.wildlifetrust.org.uk (accessed 27 May 2015).

Chapter 4: Evolution and inheritance

http://darwin200.christs.cam.ac.uk/pages/index.php?page_id=j (accessed 23 March 2015)

http://naturedocumentaries.org/category/evolution/ (accessed 5 April 2015)

www.bbc.co.uk/sn/prehistoric_life/human/human_evolution/ (accessed 2 April 2015)

Chapter 5: Everyday materials and their properties

www.periodicvideos.com/ (accessed 9 October 2015)

www.sixtysymbols.com (accessed 9 October 2015)

www.stevespanglerscience.com/experiments (accessed 9 October 2015)

www.teachersmedia.co.uk/videos/materials-activities (accessed 9 October 2015)

www.webelements.com (accessed 9 October 2015)

www.youtube.com/watch?v=9vk4_2xboOE (accessed 9 October 2015)

Chapter 6: Earth and space

http://imagine.gsfc.nasa.gov/docs/teachers/lessons/xray_spectra/background-lifecycles.html (accessed 9 October 2015)

www.cosmos4kids.com/ (accessed 9 October 2015)

www.fourmilab.ch/earthview/ (accessed 9 October 2015)

www.kidsastronomy.com/astroskymap/constellations.htm (accessed 9 October 2015)

www.kidsastronomy.com/earth.htm (accessed 9 October 2015)

www.spaceplace.nasa.gov/menu/solar-system/ (accessed 9 October 2015)

www.wikihow.com/Make-a-Sundial (accessed 9 October 2015)

www.worldtimezone.com/ (accessed 9 October 2015)

Chapter 7: Rocks

http://news.bbc.co.uk/1/hi/8398451.stm (accessed 27 July 2015)

www.bbc.co.uk/nature/14343366 (accessed 24 July 2015)

www.letswasteless.com/cms/composting.aspx (accessed 3 August 2015)

www.nhm.ac.uk/kids-only/dinosaurs/ (accessed 15 May 2015)

www.soil-net.com/primary/ (accessed 1 February 2015)

www.trilobites.info/trilobite.htm (accessed 15 March 2015)

Chapter 8: Light

www.bbc.co.uk/bitesize/ks2/science/physical_processes/light/play/ (accessed 1 February 2015)

www.bbc.co.uk/schools/teachers/ks2_lessonplans/science/see.shtml (accessed 3 February 2015)

www.cehjournal.org/resources/healthy-eyes-activity-book-for-primary-schools/ (accessed 3 February 2015)

www.explainthatstuff.com/light.html (accessed 1 February 2015)

Chapter 9: Forces, motion and magnets

www.bbc.co.uk/bitesize/ks2/science/physical_processes/forces/quiz/q74052238/ (accessed 5 April 2015)

www.bbc.co.uk/bitesize/ks2/science/physical_processes/forces/read/1/ (accessed 5 April 2015)

www.bbc.co.uk/schools/scienceclips/ages/10_11/forces_action.shtml (accessed 5 April 2015)

www.nationalstemcentre.org.uk/elibrary/search?term=forces&order=score (accessed 5 April 2015)

Chapter 10: Sound

http://homepage.eircom.net/~kogrange/sound_experiments2.html#hanginthere (accessed 3 February 2015)

www.bbc.co.uk/bitesize/ks2/science/physical_processes/sound/read/1/ (accessed 1 February 2015)

www.bbc.co.uk/schools/teachers/ks2_lessonplans/science/changing_sounds.shtml (accessed 3 February 2015)

www.sciencekids.co.nz/gamesactivities/changingsounds.html (accessed 24 February 2015)

Chapter 11: Electricity

http://learningcircuits.co.uk (accessed 9 October 2015)

www.teachersmedia.co.uk/subjects/primary/electricity-magnetism (accessed 9 October 2015)

Index

Help us to help you!

Our aim is to help you to become the best professional you can be. In order to improve your critical thinking skills we are pleased to offer you a **free booklet** on the subject. Just go to our website www.criticalpublishing.com and click the link on the home page. We have more free resources on our website which you may also find useful.

If you'd like to write a review of this book on Amazon, BooksEtc, or Wordery, **we would be happy to send you the digital version of the book for free.**

Email a link to your review to us at admin@criticalpublishing.com, and we'll reply with a PDF of the book, which you can read on your phone, tablet or Kindle.

You can also connect with us on:

Twitter	@CriticalPub	#criticalpublishing
Facebook	www.facebook.com/Critical-Publishing-456875584333404	
Our blog	https://thecriticalblog.wordpress.com	